I Love You, Mom!

FOREWORD BY
KELLY RIPA

EDITED BY
DIANE CLEHANE

I Love You, Mom!

A Celebration of Our Mothers

and Their Gifts to Us

HYPERION | NEW YORK

ISBN: 0-4013-0043-X

Hyperion books are available for special pro-
motions and premiums. For details contact
Hyperion Special Markets, 77 West 66th
Street, 11th floor, New York, New York 10023,
or call 212-456-0133.

Designed by Lorelle Graffeo

FIRST EDITION

10 9 8 7 6 5 4 3 2 1

Contents

Foreword

BY KELLY RIPA

WHAT IS IT THAT MAKES YOUR mother so wondrous? Is it that she has the ability to kiss a boo-boo and make it better? That only her toasted cheese sandwiches are melted just right? Why does a drink of water from your mother's glass taste so much better than the one you get for yourself? Why is it that moms are the first people thanked at awards shows or when sports professionals win a critical game?

The answers to all of these questions are simple. Anyone who has a mother, or anyone who longingly remembers a mother they lost, can tell you. The word *mom* embodies a person who not only is a friend, support system, and mentor; she is someone that her children can rely on at any hour of the day.

UNCONDITIONAL LOVE:

A phrase commonly overused, but completely understood by a mom. For only a mother could look into her child's eyes and adore his blue hair, pierced eyebrow, and tattooed forehead, and totally appreciate his individuality. Some may claim he has the face only a mother could love, but she will say "My son, the rock star, have you ever seen anyone wear an eyebrow ring with such style?" A mother celebrates her child's accomplishments with pride, as well as praises effort that might not have been met with achievement. Steadfastly work toward success, whether it's riding a bicycle or taking the bar exam, and both will have equal meaning and importance to a mom.

PATIENCE:

Could it be that a mom simply requires less sleep than everyone else in the universe? Why is she always awake? Especially if you're trying to sneak in past curfew or call her in the middle of the night to discuss a problem at work, or you're in bed with the chicken pox, every time you wake up, your mom is sitting by your bed just waiting to make you feel better. Moms can listen to their children wax on endlessly about anything with genuine interest, and without ever judging. (Well, hardly ever!) The advice a mom gives is steeped in knowledge, and sometimes children wisely accept the advice and follow it. When you don't, however, a mom never says, "I told you so." (Well, hardly ever!)

DEVOTION:

There has never been a bond stronger than that between a mom and her children. Any mom can easily profess that the true love of her life is her children. The timeless saying that being a mom is the toughest job one will have to do is not only accurate, but is a tremendous understatement in terms of what being a mother means. Moms tirelessly juggle the roles of teacher, doctor, therapist, cheerleader, chauffeur, disciplinarian, cook, and confidante—and receive minimal praise for their twenty-four hours a day of hard work. She will assume the role of teacher, first teaching the basics of walking and talking. She will then move on to homework, diligently checking and rechecking math equations, and finally teaching her children how to be caring parents themselves. The role of chef is one she tackles, even if she's a terrible cook. Anyone will tell you there is nothing as comforting as a home-cooked meal lovingly prepared by your mom. Whether it's a twelve-course Thanksgiving extravaganza or tomato soup from the can, if Mom made it, it's delicious.

Mom can also just as easily become the family taxi driver, shuttling her kids to and from school, to after-school activities, even on first dates (as uncool as that may seem at the time). Let's not forget the family security guard, for no one ever keeps as watchful an eye on her children as a mom does. At the park, grocery store, mall, or front lawn, the eyes of a mom are never far away, protecting her kids sternly from themselves, or fiercely from strangers if need be.

Moms selflessly assume these vastly different challenging roles, and seldom receive credit for their unrelenting care. From the middle-of-the-night wake-up calls to cleaning up bathroom mishaps, moms perform these sometimes unpleasant tasks with sustained love and care.

It is with these thoughts and appreciations that the spirit of this book was created, giving people the opportunity to simply say, "Thanks, Mom," for the millions of hours of unconditional love, patience, devotion, and indentured servitude that for the most part until now has gone unthanked. Stories are shared of countless acts of kindness, as well as humorous tales and serious stories of strength in dealing with illness, divorce, and death. In addition, there are inspirational stories of triumph over adversity, and success after failure.

Contributors to this book share their life experiences that everyone can relate to, and the one common denominator in every story is that theirs is a great mother responsible for the actor, writer, athlete, singer, or politician writing their notes of thanks. Whether she's your inspiration, your best friend, your psychologist, teacher, fashion consultant, hairdresser, or even occasional enemy, she's your mom—and she is the greatest person you know, the person you aspire to be the most like, and the person who will forever offer her unwavering support.

The
Favorite
Son

LARRY KING

Broadcaster

My mother lost a son who died of a
burst appendix before I was born.
Then she lost her husband when I
was nine and a half years old and
her mother two weeks later. So she
raised her two boys, my younger
brother and me, alone. She loved
my younger brother very much, but
I was her life—I was certainly the
favorite child. In the morning, she'd
say, "So, for dinner, what do we

want, boys?" I'd say, "Lamb chops," and my brother would say, "Chicken." We'd have lamb chops.

When she went down to Miami and lived the last years of her life there and she saw me attain some degree of success there, my picture with all these famous people was all over the walls in her home. My brother graduated cum laude from St. John's and made Law Review. I never went to college. But my brother loved her very much—you couldn't help but love her. She was a dear, dear woman.

She was very doting and remained doting. All of her sisters' (she was one of six) children went to college. I was kind of the black sheep of the family. I was working at odd jobs until I broke into broadcasting, but she stood by me. She used to rave about me to all the relatives. Nothing really changed as I grew up. If I had a failed marriage, it was the woman's fault. It was never my fault. I lost a tooth when I was eleven and I just didn't want to go to the dentist. So because I didn't want to go, we didn't go and I never replaced the tooth and wound up having tooth problems because she didn't drag me to the dentist. She should have, but she didn't because I didn't want to go. If I blew up a bank and they came to my mother, she might have said, "They probably made a mistake in his checking account. They shouldn't have bothered my Label [that's the Jewish name for Lawrence]." I never got a major reprimand from her.

I inherited many fine qualities from her. She had intense loyalty that I know I inherited from her. It's the attribute I admire most. My best friends are people I've known since I was nine and ten years old—and they knew my mother. She valued family, and even though I've had failed marriages, I've been a very good step-father and am currently a good father. My mother was not a tight-wad and I'm not a tightwad.

More than anything else, she was always there for my brother and me. There are no instances in my life where she let me down. If she said she was going to do something, she did it. She'd offer her opinion but was never pressing. I never heard her say, "You *must* do that." She was more of a good listener. She was totally supportive of my wanting to go into broadcasting. She never said, "Why don't you go into something else?"

She never got to see me go national. She died in 1976. I went national in 1978. I don't think she would believe it, the fact that her son was being seen where she grew up, in Minsk, Russia—she would flip. She would not be able to comprehend the money I make, the house I live in, the family I have. I think about her all the time. I don't believe in an afterlife; I'm an agnostic but I know she is still with me. Every time I see my brother, he says, "Did you think of Mommy today?" and I say, "I sure did." Things happen all the time that make me think of her—expressions I think of and things I see, and a flash will just occur to me or someone cooks me something that tastes like something she made. She was a great Jewish cook who took pride in her kitchen. All meat was well done and to this day I hate red meat. Another thing she inbred in me was that in a kosher home you don't mix dairy and meat. To this day, I can't have meat and milk. It would curdle my stomach. If I ate a hamburger with a glass of milk, I'd faint.

I quote my mother a lot—"Who knew?"—she said that all the time. Little Yiddish expressions she said, I use a lot. I think the greatest lesson she taught me was to never quit. Even during those down-and-out moments of my life when things looked bleak, she was an optimist. She'd always say, "Don't worry, Label, you're the best!" She taught me optimism and that's a very valuable trait in my field. She was an up person. I wish she were here. You can never replace your mother. And no matter how old you get, you never stop missing her.

Legacy
of Love

JANE CLAYSON

Broadcast Journalist

I remember the moment when I first respected and appreciated my mom as a person—not as someone I looked up to because I was a little girl and she was the mom. It was when my little brother, David, was diagnosed with a brain tumor. I was seventeen and a senior in high school, which is an awkward time for moms and daughters anyway. Our relationship evolved in a very unique way that year because I was forced to put away teenage problems and insecurities—What am I going to wear to school tomorrow? Which friends am I going to go to the party with on Friday night?—because the bigger, more significant issues of life were staring me right in the face.

I remember thinking if I could ever have the strength and compassion that this woman does, I will have lived a good life. I'll never forget seeing her twenty-four hours a day, seven days a week at David's bedside. He was just eleven. David couldn't speak, he could barely move. This very loving mother would go through the alphabet letter by letter and David would open his eyes when the right letter came along—they would spell words this way. That is how they communicated. To this day, I still consider that to be the most extraordinary example of compassion I have ever seen.

David was sick for about a year and finally he died just two days before Christmas. It took me a long time to get over David's death, but I think as a mother you never fully recover from the loss of a child. I can't imagine that you're ever the same. She's still the one who, on Christmas or on his birthday, will include him with a little prayer or a thoughtful remembrance. It shows an incredible amount of love—a mother's love.

She has shown that same unconditional love to me. My mom started writing me little notes and cards from the time I was just a little girl. I would keep them in a shoebox under my bed. As the years have gone by, the shoeboxes have become bigger boxes—

and I have many of them. If I was down, I'd get a "Cheer Up" kind of card. If I was sick, I'd find a "Get Well" note in my mailbox. She'd send them on birthdays and holidays. In fact, I'd get them all the time—and not just cards and letters. She'd send what I called little "love packets"—nothing expensive. She'd say, "I saw this frame in the Hallmark store and I thought you might like it" or "The last time you came home I noticed your pajamas looked a little ratty . . . so here's a new pair I found at the store today." The thoughtful things that only a mom can do.

One of the most significant gifts my mom gave to me was the gift of music. She is a violinist, and when she was in college, she performed as a soloist on USO tours. Years later, she would inspire her children with her passion. I started playing when I was six. Soon enough, both my sister and brother joined in and we had a quartet. Our favorite piece was Vivaldi's Concerto for Four Violins. My dad would accompany us on the piano. Sure, there were plenty of sour notes, but it was something that brought us closer together as a family . . . all inspired by my mother. I once had a violin teacher who said, "You can't succeed unless you have a 'Violin Momma'—someone who will believe in you, someone who will sit and practice with you, even when you don't want to do it." Well, there were plenty of knock-down-drag-outs when I didn't want to practice! But it was a discipline she thought was important. And now, as an adult, I look back and I thank her.

Abraham Lincoln once said, "I am who I am because of my angel mother." I feel that way—I am who I am because of my angel mother. She is always there, supporting me, encouraging me, *believing* in me. I remember when I moved to New York City to anchor *The Early Show* on CBS. It was exciting and exhilarating and overwhelming all at the same time. I was in The Big City—a new and different world. My parents came from California to help me unpack and get settled. I remember the day before I started that broadcast, my mom said, "Let's go out and celebrate. We'll take you anywhere you want to go in the city for a good-luck meal to get you on your way." The first thought that came to my mind was, "The only thing I want to do right now is be with my mom and eat her tuna fish sandwiches, which are my very favorite thing in the world." So, my mom went out and bought the ingredients—I had nothing in my barren kitchen. And that night we sat on the floor of my unfurnished apartment and ate tuna fish sandwiches.

I never felt more love in my whole life than at that moment.

Heart
&
Sole

MELISSA RIVERS

Television Host

I think the thing I most appreciate about my mother is her sense of loyalty. She's never, ever not been there for me. That's just the way she is. She might have disagreed with me on a certain decision I was making, but once I commit to that decision, she will always stand behind it.

She was just a parent to me when I was growing up, now she also wears the hat of friend and confidante. Working together has changed the relationship we have because now she wears a third hat—which is coworker. Sometimes it's hard to switch gears, but we always manage to. We talk almost every day. This morning we were talking about my son, Cooper, and our dogs—there's nothing we don't talk about. Now that I'm a mother I'm amazed at how she juggled everything, because I never felt denied anything in terms of time and attention. As a working mother I ask myself, "How the heck did she do all that and never make me feel like I was an imposition?" I have a whole new respect for her now.

The best advice she has ever given me is to never give up. She believes when one door shuts, another door opens. Always, always move forward. I admire her tenacity and her generosity and her ability to do seventeen things at once.

We had to reconnect as adults on a totally new level after my father's suicide and learn how to deal with each other in a different way. We both had a lot of things we had to accept about each other and who we were as people rather than just being parent and child. It was a different experience having to deal with that and with my mother having different emotions and feelings. There was also having to deal with her dating again, which was an eye-opener—I think just recently have I been able to deal with it a little better now that I've begun dating again myself.

My mom taught me how to be a survivor. But most important, my mom gave me a sense of humor and taught me how to laugh at myself and sometimes to just not take it all so seriously. She showed me how to wake up every day and appreciate how great your life is. Whenever I get into trouble, I think to myself, "Love, faith, courage," and that comes from her.

I'd like to thank my mother for giving me several things. First, thanks, Mom, for giving me the courage to never, ever stay there when I get knocked down, and to get back up. Second, thank you for the ability to give and receive love. I find that so much with my son. He gives it so freely and you just have to be able to accept it, and that's a really hard thing for me. It's only now that I'm starting to say it's okay to let people be nice. And finally, thank you for giving me the faith to believe in myself and knowing that no matter what happens I'm going to be okay.

Just recently I was under a lot of pressure at work and my personal life was a disaster. I was very down and feeling like I wasn't going to come out of it. Out of the blue, she said to me, "I'm really proud of how you're handling yourself." And I thought, if I'm making her proud of me, then I'm going to be okay. She renewed my faith in myself and my decisions.

I have a tremendous amount of respect for what my mother has accomplished professionally and what she's survived as a person—and of course, I admire her fashion sense. The one thing I regret is that my foot is bigger than hers, so I can't get into any of her Manolo Blahniks.

The Girl
in the
Cat Suit

BILL BROCHTRUP

Actor

When my father's father, Clarence, died a few years ago, I found, in a suitcase in his garage, an old, faded, heart-shaped valentine candy box filled with letters he had written to my grandmother, Betty, in 1925. They were not full of poetry and declarations of love, but simple letters talking about how he hoped he'd get a chance to see her next weekend, about what his brothers were up to, about how if he could get time off from work he would try to make the drive all the way from Los Angeles to Inglewood (maybe a fifteen-minute drive on today's freeways) to visit her. Just the things a twenty-five-year-old guy might say to a girl he liked.

When my mother's mother died this past year, I found a box in her hall closet that held a very similar collection of letters, written by my grandfather Ken to my grandmother Grace in 1926. Although his spelling was a bit worse, and his tone a little more randy, the letters were very much the same. He had been working construction on a hotel in Arizona, missed her, and had been razzed by the other fellows because "his girl" didn't write too often. And they had gotten drunk at a rodeo in Mexico over the weekend. He was hoping to see her back in L.A. soon.

These letters made me start to realize the disconcerting fact that I really didn't know these grandparents as *people*. Of course I knew them very well as my ninis and papas (as my sisters and I called them). They all lived long lives and we spent plenty of time with them. But the perspective was always that of a grandkid, never of a peer. Looking through Nini's 1926 Inglewood High yearbook (which I also found in the box in the closet), I wondered who she really *was*—was she a party girl? The quiet one? The clown? Those letters made me think about the difficulty of truly knowing our relatives from the perspective of equals, as peers. The kids in those letters had hopes and dreams and senses of humor and private jokes about which I knew nothing.

Which brings me to my own mother, Carolyn. She was born here in Los Angeles at the end of World War II, went to high school with the Frankie and Annette beach crowd, met my father, Bill, and married young. She was only nineteen when I was born, and by the time she was twenty-six, she had four kids.

That's the kind of thing I am talking about—I have a photo of my second Halloween. I am dressed in a little tiger suit, and my mother is dressed the same. I see a picture of me and my mom. It is harder for me to see a picture of a twenty-one-year-old girl dressed as a large cat.

I don't know, from her point of view, the details of how she raised us (I suppose I could ask, but explanation is not the same as true understanding)—how did she manage all those diapers? What were my parents thinking having my youngest two sisters eleven months apart? How hard was it to leave behind their own parents when we left California and moved up to Washington State? Did they really have a good time when we took the summer and drove around the country, camping in a Winnebago? Did she really think she could fool us by baking "healthy" carob-chip cookies? How much fun could it really be to go backpacking in the rain of Mount Rainier with four whiny children and two pup tents?

I *can* say that my mother's influence is strong. She shaped so much of the way I now perceive the world. I rather incorrectly use the term *normal* to describe things our family did, that I simply assume all families do. As in, "Don't all normal people make stuffing with the giblets?" Or, "Don't all normal people lounge on the floor?" Or, "All normal people play cards."

I've learned that everything my mother says has turned out to be true. When you are depressed, it really does help to eat right and get more exercise. Fudge truly is impossible to make. She really doesn't care what I do, as long as it makes me happy.

My mother is sporty—she coached the eighth-grade girls at my Catholic school to softball victory. She taught me what you need in a good second baseman. She is artistic—she has made stained glass, won photography prizes, and went through a severe pottery stage. She is athletic, and has boxes of equestrian trophies to prove it. She is bright and bold; she went back to college and graduated the same year I finished high school. She is embracing of me, and my friends, and my sisters' friends, and strays of all kinds—and understands that a family is made up of whoever wants to join it. She is a more-the-merrier mom. She is adventuresome and well traveled—she explored Egypt, Mongolia, and Thailand. She is competitive. I would love to be eavesdropping at the next table in an all-night buffet in Vegas when she and I have had some serious discussions about the play of certain numbers on the roulette wheel (I am obsessed by 22 and 23, she prefers 29 and that awful 0/00).

And she has succeeded at what I believe she would consider her most important goal. She (and my father, don't forget him) has been able to create a family that is so close, loving, and together it's virtually impossible for us to imagine it being any other way.

As I've gotten older, my mother and I have come to know each other as people, as peers, as friends. All my life my friends have thought my mom was really fun, very cool. She is. More and more I know that for myself.

A Mother's Love

MAX VON ESSEN

Actor

My mother, Rita, and I have an extremely close relationship that has just gotten better over the years. She is the glue that holds our family together. This was never more evident than on September 11, 2001. My father, Thomas von Essen, spent his career in the New York City Fire Department and held the post of Fire Commissioner when the towers came down. In an instant our family lost our closest friends and my father's longest-term colleagues. My mom immediately took time off from work and was at my dad's side at every moment. Her selflessness at this difficult time overwhelmed us all. As the backbone of our family, she helped us through an extremely traumatic year.

My family has always been animated, expressive, and highly emotional. I guess that has something to do with my mom's Italian heritage. My dad comes from a somewhat stoic German background where emotions are more guarded. I think that difference is one of the things he loves so much about my mom and what drew him to her in the first place. When we were kids, if we misbehaved, my mom would reach toward her foot, pull off a stylish high heel, and start yelling. This action clearly meant, stop it, or the shoe goes flying! We would have to do something almost unimaginable to see that heel go flying, but you can be sure there were two or three occasions where it was airborne. Even though my family was expressive and willing to wear emotions on our sleeves, we still wouldn't necessarily talk about our feelings or dig into things. As my siblings and I mature, I realize more and more that that flying shoe and the person it came from has allowed us to be more open with each other.

My mother is who she is. She never tries to hide anything. She's honest and unafraid to express her emotions. Actors spend years in training to do this. I'm lucky enough to have had a head start because of my mother!

I think my mom and I are best friends. I am completely comfortable being myself with her. We live near each other and meet once a week or more at the local diner for breakfast or for a little shopping. It's nice to have someone supportive and totally on my side. It's a bonus that it's my mom! After graduating from college with an economics degree, I planned on coming to New York to work on Wall Street. I was fearful of following my true dream, which was to pursue acting. I was a little nervous about talking to my dad about it. I mean, he always supported my interest in the arts, but I also got the sense he thought it was a wonderful hobby and not necessarily the wisest career choice. I remember talking to my mother about it and she said, "Go with your heart. If that's what you love, how can you not pursue it?" As it turned out, my father was in total agreement. So that was it. I've never looked back, and I've been lucky enough to work as an actor consistently and with much success. All those years of piano, voice, and acting lessons where Mom schlepped me from place to place have paid off!

When I did my first Broadway show, *Jesus Christ Superstar,* I played an apostle as well as the standby for Jesus. I had the opportunity to play Jesus often and it was great to have my mom in the audience. The first time she came to see me in that production, my sister said that Mom was so nervous and excited that she almost removed herself from the audience. Later that evening, my sister told me that she was surprised that Mom did make it through the performance, especially given the intensity of the crucifixion scene. I mean, what mom can sit through seeing her son crucified? But she did. And she did it at least twelve more times. She has since seen me in other shows where my characters meet a similar fate. (Why do I always get hired for the guy who comes to a tragic ending?!) Despite the fact that it's torturous for her to see me in pain and anguish even on stage, my mother is always there. I'm currently starring in the Broadway show *Dance of the Vampires*. I don't die! I feel as if it's sort of a gift to Mom. She can actually enjoy the show without worrying about my safety on stage.

My mother is loving and giving. She leads her life by example. She's an amazing woman and I love her with all my heart. I'm proud to be my mother's son.

Reality Checks

FINOLA HUGHES

Actress

"Look both ways when crossing the street or you'll wake up next Sunday as a hood ornament." Sage advice offered up by my mother when I was about five and learning to navigate London traffic.

Perhaps unwise and certainly unorthodox was her comment to "take a comic book" after I had complained about the lengthy sermons delivered at our local church. One time I asked why a brightly dressed woman was standing on a street corner with a small dog. "That's a prostitute, dear," I was informed. I don't know whether she was or not, as I was eight years old at the time. The woman could have easily been waiting for a bus.

When I entered a new school for the first time, she said, "Do your own thing and don't mind the other kids and don't bite." I was ten.

When I failed to remember to feed my guinea pig and the poor thing expired through lack of interest, my mother gave me a hug as I sobbed and said, "As much as we love *The Tales of Beatrix Potter,* guinea pigs are unable to go shopping for themselves."

When my little brother was born she said, "Hold him against your heart." And I have, Mom, for thirty-four years so far.

One birthday she took me into a jeweler's shop and bought me a chain on which she placed a crucifix and a Star of David. "All religions are equal, as are all people," she told me. I wore it proudly and still have it tucked away in a jewelry box somewhere.

Things that bored her she had very little time for. "Let's not do the housework, let's go see a ballet instead." I was all for that, as my room was like an obstacle course. When I turned into a horrible teenager she'd bark, "Read a book, don't dribble about."

When I started going out with boys she said, "The best advice I can give you about men is to have your own car and your own apartment." I was fourteen and that seemed such a distant dream when all I wanted was a glance from Gary Shale!

When I moved away from home she told me, "Work hard, love fiercely." I have tried to, every day.

My mom was amused by the world she lived in and she left it much too soon. She always made me laugh, even her brutal honesty was delivered with a grin. Perhaps on the outside she appeared to be a tiger; however, her cuddles were those of a pussycat.

There are no words to say how much I would thank her if I could. I would write it on a butterfly wing and send it into the sky. Mom, you'd be happy to know I still don't bite and I try never to do housework!

Mommy
Mary

**CATHERINE
HICKLAND**

Actress

My mother is coming up on her eightieth birthday and what I hear most from my friends is, "Wow, your mom doesn't look eighty!" I couldn't agree more. In my eyes, she still looks exactly the same as when I was five years old and looked up to the woman who taught me so much about everything. I don't see a wrinkle.

Moms have enough to worry about, but my parents were divorced when I was only five, and I imagine my mother had it really hard raising two girls alone. She had many, many hardships, but still managed to instill the values of love, hard work, and being there for others. It isn't easy to discipline your kids without guilt, but she managed, and sometimes the discipline was really tough. We lived in a rough neighborhood, so it was doubly difficult to keep track of two teenage girls—and our curfew was strict. Of course, my sister and I hated that. We were always mad at her because it seemed so much more severe than our friends' curfews. Of course we complained to each other, but we were home at the designated time because she was *the boss*.

Looking back now, I am so grateful. So many of the kids I grew up with didn't live to see twenty-two or they didn't have any focus or direction in their lives. They settled for less than they wanted out of life. They didn't dream, so they didn't achieve. My mother always supported my dream of being an actress. She never said I couldn't do it, so I just naturally assumed I could. She never discouraged me from entering contests or auditioning for high school musicals, and she came to every single one I was in—and believe me, there were many!

In the middle of my childhood, my mother had an emotional breakdown; the financial stress and pressure of raising two kids alone became too much. She had to take a little time off, so my grandmother took over for a while. It was then that my sister, brother (who was raised by my grandmother), and I had the chance to see what can happen to a person if they are not able to ask for help when they need it (which, I think, is a difficult thing for girls to do anyway). It wasn't long before she bounced back. We were back to normal before we knew it. This experience taught me compassion and not to expect perfection from anyone but myself. And if I can't do something perfectly, that's okay too, as long as I've done it to the best of my ability. We are flawed and we are still beautiful.

I love you, Mom. You are a hero to me.

The Greatest Gift

EVA LA RUE

Actress

My mom became a single mom when I was seven and my parents divorced. It was just me, my mom, and my sister, Nika. Growing up, I always felt like we were "the Three Musketeers." My dad always gave what he could in child support, but they were both really broke and we basically grew up on welfare. I specifically remember a few times when our main delicacy was anything made with Bisquick and water.

A single mom's life is anything but easy. But economic hardship is nothing compared to the heartache my mother endured when my older brother, Chuck, was killed by a drunk driver. After that, I think my mom got a lot of strength from us, and was more acutely aware of how precious every day with her children was.

When I was little I thought she was the most multitalented, creative person in the world. She was so good with us, nurturing whatever talents we had and supporting all the things we loved to do. She was never negative about anything we wanted to try. My mom would always try to discover what we were talented at, and even though there was never any extra money, she would find a way for us to do it. Once she even picked up a weekend job at an ice-skating rink in exchange for lessons for us. She gave up everything for us and she is totally responsible for me being a performer. She got my sister and me into children's theater; she drove us an hour and a half each way to dance class five days a week and all without complaint! She made sure I got an education through scholarships—I was on different ones for ten years. She did all that, and was always working two or three jobs at a time—everything from working in a mailroom to working at a plastics company. And at one point, we had ten paper routes! For a year, our living room was dedicated to thousands of newspapers to be stuffed into those little plastic bags. The three of us were elbow deep in black news ink!

No matter what the job, she always tried to be there for us when we got home.

I don't think I really saw my mom as a complete individual person until I had my daughter, Kaya. I never realized that, of course, she had had her own hopes and dreams at one time, and had given them up to focus on making sure her kids could have a better life. I just didn't appreciate as a child how much time and energy it took for her to do that, that she really did the best she could with what she had financially and emotionally. I know now that there were times when she didn't want to get in that car and drive us to dance class or to the theater, but she always did. I love my baby with all my heart and would do anything for her, but I don't know if I could do it with the same gleam in my eye. I guess it takes becoming a mom to fully appreciate your mom—because now I call her constantly to say, "I don't know how you did it!"

Mother-daughter relationships are complicated. During my teen years, I gave my mom quite a run for her money while I was trying to establish my independence. Oh, the screaming matches! The kind every mother wishes on her daughter when she has her own teen—as silent revenge!

When I became an adult, we went through another transition when she had to learn to let go. I think one of the hardest parts of being a mother is trying to figure out where you end and your child begins. They come from us, but they don't belong to us, and in the end, you have to step back and trust that they will find their own way, mistakes and all. God help me when that day comes for me—and I'm sure it will come faster than I think. I only hope that I can step away with the same love, support, and understanding my mother had. As hard as it was for her, I think she knows that her love guides me daily whether we are together or apart. There are really no words to express the unconditional love, gratitude, and appreciation I feel for my mom, the person who taught me to go confidently in the direction of my dreams— dreams that have been realized because of her.

A Recipe
for
Happiness

COLIN COWIE

Author/Television Host

My mother is without doubt one of the closest people to me in my life. Although she lives in South Africa, we speak almost daily. I am the youngest in the family, and when I was twelve my father passed away. As a result of his death, we became very close when I was young. It took many years for my mother to overcome the loss of my father. Theirs was a great love story.

The two of us are uncannily alike. I inherited her fabulously dry sense of humor and find myself in situations where I realize we act exactly the same way. We tend to use the same sayings— it's as if it's instinctual.

Living in Zambia in Central Africa when I was growing up, we didn't have malls and multiplex movie theaters. We had one country club, one hotel, and one restaurant, so I can't recall a time when we didn't have houseguests or people for cocktails or tea on a Sunday afternoon. It was a very social life in our home. One day when I was about ten years old, I remember being punished and told to go help in the kitchen. I've never left, and today I've built an empire out of entertaining.

When I was a teenager I was somewhat rebellious, but I always appreciated my mom's companionship. Even now I get emotional when she visits, which is once a year in either New York or Los Angeles, depending on where I'm working at the time. She stays for about a month, sometimes longer if I'm lucky. We love to spend time together shopping, dining out, or just catching up with one another, alone or with my friends. Since my mother's been visiting me for the past eighteen years, she's had the chance to meet almost all of my friends. All of them adore her, and she them.

I'm very proud to share my accomplishments with my mother, and although I send home the occasional clippings or video, it's wonderful to have her with me where she can see firsthand what I do. She's always been supportive of whatever I've chosen to pursue and has never tried to force me into doing something I didn't want to do. She's always guided me forward and always gives me unconditional love and support. Completely. It's the basis of our true friendship.

My mother has the wonderful gift of looking at any situation and identifying five things that are beautiful before finding one at fault. I have a slightly edited version of that gift, but I try to be as much like her as possible. She's taught me so much about patience, tenacity, love, and acceptance. She encourages me to travel, experience life, and always go the extra mile. I hold not a secret from her and try to listen to her wisdom.

I travel home to South Africa for two to three weeks each year. The first time I left home, I went into the military at sixteen for two years of mandatory service. From there I moved to Johannesburg and five years later I immigrated to the United States. So basically I've been away from home longer than I actually lived there, but somehow, no matter where I am, even in the military operational zone, I manage to phone my mother just to hear her voice. Often I'll call and she'll say, "I was just thinking of you." And I'll say, "I got the message."

In every book I've written I always end the acknowledgments with a word of gratitude to my mother. I thank her for teaching me to live my life with great passion and unquestioned integrity. She's instilled in me the values of a gentleman and has taught me what's important in life. She's guided me along the way and continues to support me unconditionally. She's a true friend.

My Mentor

MARIA
CUOMO COLE

Activist

My relationship with my mother has evolved into a great friendship. Today, she is a mentor and a guide to me. There's a unique bond that women with children have with their mothers. When I had children it added a whole new dimension to our relationship. For the first time, I was able to relate to her as a woman instead of just as a mother. My mother has wonderful instincts about people and life and has a fine barometer on the current situation and a course to take. She never succumbs to the petty. She always reminds me of the better path, whether that relates to parenting or personal decisions. I find myself increasingly taking her advice.

She has an effective way of acting as my children's advocate and as a grandmother seeing the child's perspective in a way I don't know she could have possibly been able to as a mother. In turn, my children really confide in her. One of my daughters loves opera. She's in the Children's Met Choir and after her opera class will call my parents and they will tell her every opera singer that ever sang the particular aria she just sang. In that way, too, my mother is able to enrich that experience for my daughter. When it comes to anything in the fine arts, she is just this incredible source of knowledge.

When I was growing up, she was a busy mother with five children and a husband with a very full work world that she shared with him, so she was pulled in many directions. I certainly appreciate that now. My father had a very demanding schedule and traveled a lot and spent a great deal of time away from our home, particularly in the early years of his career. My mother was always the constant in our lives. As busy as she was, she invested the time and the sensitivity into being the best mother to each individual child that she could be— which I personally think is the art of motherhood. She nurtured our individual interests, talents, and passions—somehow she found the time to do all of that. I'm still not quite sure how she did it.

As I got older, she was very empowering. She drove me to ballet classes, Girl Scouts, and swim team practice. She didn't have a nanny—she did everything herself. She did have a terrific support system of neighborhood stay-at-home mothers who all helped one another. Not a week goes by when my mother doesn't say to me, "Isn't there somebody you can carpool with?" She finds it hard to believe sometimes I am truly stuck.

I have learned a great deal from my mother's relentless dedication—she's such a committed person and an extraordinarily dedicated mother. She really invested her time and her priorities in her children's best interests. She was a very active person—involved in our school, in our community, in the greater community, and in our church. One of the things I've grown to appreciate more and more is her investment in our pleasure and enrichment—especially when it came to the holidays, nature, and food. We were a religious Catholic family, so our religious observances were very important and she would make them meaningful and really integrate them into our lives instead of just having us mark an occasion. She did it in a multisensory way by involving us in the creative processes, whether it was making cupcakes or decorating the house for Christmas. As part of the process we actually talked about the occasion. Often we're all so busy that we celebrate these rituals in a perfunctory way, but perhaps we don't really celebrate their essence. Now I try to create those traditions for my children.

I talk to my mother every day and it's really that *I* want to speak to *her*. I speak to both my parents every day. She's my first call in the morning and often my last at night. She's very proud of my work. As an adult I have been able to collaborate with her and learn from her efforts in a clear way. She has always been very committed to issues related to children and family, and participated in a number of community initiatives for children. When my father was elected governor of New York in 1982, my mother created the first mentoring initiative in New York State—she's really a pioneer in mentoring. She persevered in developing the programs she felt met the needs of New York's at-risk children. Today, there's a foster care initiative in place, and that was a long-term goal of hers.

At the same time she has been this unstoppable force in her work, she has been this delightful, joyful person with an infectious sense of humor. She's someone who makes everyone around her feel good. Remarkably, she and my father are the only two people I know who have remained absolutely pure, considering their journey. They've shared an interesting, trying, rewarding, blessed journey—as a family we all have. They have remained idealistic. I believe my mother is really an angel of mercy. There is not a person in need that she encounters that she does not go out of her way to help. She's incredible in that way. My mother has been a constant reminder to me to stay true to my passion, interests, and dreams. She taught me to persevere in meeting your professional goals while as a parent keeping your home life your number one priority.

Happy Days

JACKLYN ZEMAN

Actress

My relationship with my mother has always been one of the most important relationships—if not *the* most important relationship of my life. I count myself so lucky to say that because my mother has been the foundation of who I am. She created what was safe for me and what—to this day—is "normal" for me. My whole concept of what a person who wants a good, positive, happy life does comes from my mother. That's the gift my mother gave me, and it's a gift of great value. As a result of that, it's what I strive to give my children.

I lived in the same house in New Jersey I was born in with my parents until I moved out when I went to college. Mom is remarried and lives in Florida now. Sounds quaint to say, but we were the 1950s TV version of a happy family—I had two sisters, a mom and dad, and a dog, and we lived in the suburbs. My dad worked for IBM and my mother was a homemaker, so she was there with me every day. She cooked three meals a day. She sewed a lot of our clothes when we were kids. A family adventure was to go to New York City to see the Rockettes or go to see a Broadway show once in a while. It was a beautiful, somewhat sheltered life because all of our needs were taken care of. Both of my parents were very responsible, so as a kid, I had a very happy life.

When I was a kid, my mother was the one I would count on for most things. I remember one time walking home from elementary school, and she wasn't home. The back and front doors were locked—which we never really did in our neighborhood. I didn't have a key. I remember getting really upset and panicky— she wasn't there! I was crying and yelling and I went into the backyard and got a big stick and started hitting the back door. I knew it wasn't going to open the door, but being in third grade, I didn't know what else to do. It turned out she had gotten stuck in the snow and she had to wait until someone came to help her.

It couldn't have been more than twenty minutes that she wasn't there. When I think back to this moment now, I realize nowadays most moms aren't home—they work. There's day care, child care, car pools. I realize now how much she did—for that memory to be the one time I can think of when she wasn't there. It's amazing.

My grandma, her mother, would take the bus out one day a week from Fairview, New Jersey. She didn't drive. We thought we were so hip and happening because my mother *did* drive. We had only one car and my dad took it to work, so when we were little she had to walk to the grocery store with us in the stroller.

While my mother was always extremely supportive of what I did, I knew when I was a little girl that by her example my choices were going to be different. Internally in how I relate to things and the values she gave me, she and I are a perfect match, but it manifested itself differently. I vowed, "I'm never going to stay home and not have a car. I'm never going to let the man make all the major decisions." My mother and father's relationship was that she took care of the kids and the home; he earned the money and took care of the yard. They had very defined roles, so I grew up thinking that all men earned the money and paid the bills, and all women stayed home. I remember saying to my grandma for years, "Grandma, why don't you learn to drive? You wouldn't have to take the bus." She'd say, "I like the bus." I could never understand that. When I was young, the goal was to go to school and do well, so you would marry well and you wouldn't have to work. The pretty girls were really lucky, and if you were reasonably attractive and smart, you'd do well in life because of who you were going to get married to eventually.

My mother tells me this story about a conclusion I came to when I was eight years old. She remembers that I said, "When I grow up I'm not going to get married to someone who is going to pay for everything. I'm going to have my own money and make my own decisions." I don't recall it, but I remember the second I was old enough to baby-sit. I felt powerful when I had my own money. My mother taught me that we all appreciate so much more what we earn than what's handed to us.

She gave me so much, but the one quality that we both have—we're both a little like German shepherds in that we like to herd everybody together. We like when the whole family is in the same room. Growing up, we had a fireplace in the living room of our house, and we'd put these big chartreuse cushions in front of it and we'd roast marshmallows in front of the fire. My mother would always say those were her happiest times—when the whole family was together, the five of us and our dog.

My mother is very dependable, very reliable. She taught me about responsibility—that you honor your commitments. When you say you're going to do something, you do it. She was a Sunday school teacher, so we lived by the Ten Commandments and the "golden rule." The first and foremost thing that she taught me was always treat other people the way you want them to treat you, and if you are that way to every person you meet, you won't have a problem. She never said the word *karma*, but there was always that implication—that what goes around, comes around.

I'd like to think that I do treat other people the way I'd like them to treat me, and I've told my children it's important for them to do this too. Another thing is my mother has a very positive attitude—she's not a complainer. She's not a whiner. She used to say to us, "Don't whine, don't complain, don't be poking each other. Be nice. Be polite." Appropriate behavior was always very important to her. What I say to my kids as a result of my mother's influence is, "The most important power in the universe is the power of decision. Every day when you get up, you can make it a good day or you can make it a day that's filled with problems, so choose wisely." And it seems to have worked well with them so far.

So any time my kids have a disagreement and there's a bit of "She said this and she said that," I say to them, "You know what? You don't get to choose for someone else. You only choose for yourself. Don't be judgmental of someone else's behavior. Fix yourself and you'll be better off." My mother having taught me that has given me strength of character. Hopefully I'll do the same for my children.

It wasn't until I became a mother that I began to realize how much my mother has done for me. I don't think I've ever told her how grateful I am for all the little things she did. And now that I'm a mom I realize that the little things are really big important things. It's the everyday thoughtfulness that matters. I said "please" and "thank you" because my mother taught me that's what you do when you have good manners, but I don't think it ever really occurred to me the amount of time and energy that went into what she did for my sisters and me. My mother was not only my mother; she was also my most trusted confidante. Whether it was something that came up at school, or something was bothering me, or the day I first got my period, I would go to my mom. When I had boy problems later on, I felt safe to go to her because I respected her advice. Yet at the time I don't think I said "thank you." Because she never complained or nudged me to say thank you to her, I never realized how much she did until I had my own kids.

I laugh when I hear women joke about becoming their mothers because I think, "My goodness, I'm becoming my mother. Thank you!" She's the coolest person I've ever met.

Letter to My Mom

KELLY RIPA

Host of *Live with Regis and Kelly*

Dear Mom,

To begin to express gratitude for a person who is literally responsible for my life seems a daunting task on paper. You made sacrifices without my ever knowing it, you listened for hours on end, loved me unconditionally, and have supported all of my endeavors—and did it with grace, dignity, and beauty. You taught me what it was to be a woman, and since the moment that I was born, you are the person that I looked up to. Where do I begin to thank you and explain to you how appreciative I am? I suppose at the beginning.

My earliest memories are of watching *Dark Shadows* with you; I reveled in the late-night times we shared together. I partially think that I enjoyed staying up late because I had you to myself and we could laugh for hours. I remember when Linda, my sister, was born, you took time to buy me a book so I would feel included and special. And I remember thinking how much more beautiful I thought you were than anyone I had ever seen, even the glamorous women from *Charlie's Angels* and *Love Boat*.

Growing up, I knew that I could count on you for any obstacle that I faced. I could depend on you to drop off my homework at school when I left it at home, drive me around to all of my activities, or even tell me my hair looked great when it was sprayed and teased to at least five feet in the air! Of course, we had our difficult times during the teen years, but you always tried to understand where I was coming from. You chose to speak to me with respect and compassion, which is a skill that I try to employ with my own children. No one understands, or listens, or lends comfort the way you do. You're my best friend, and have been for my entire life. You have always been there for me when I needed you. You're the first person I call when I have good news or need advice, and of course you're the first person I call when I need consolation.

You always put us first and yourself last, doing without things so that your daughters could have everything life had to offer. However, you never acknowledged the sacrifices, as material possessions mean so little to you. Without question, your children were your top priority. Now that I am a mom, I understand all the time that you had to give up so that you could be there for ballet classes, rehearsals, or school shows. I also understand that it is not a sacrifice but a gift; not only to be able to attend such important events in a child's life but to have such a wonderful relationship is the largest blessing.

You taught us by example so many valuable life lessons, and how to appreciate the important things in life like family, health, and love. You have guided us through life with such unyielding support and pride, I always know how loved I am. My only hope is that I am the mother for my children that you have been to me. I had the best teacher, after all. So much good advice was given to me over the years, and some of it I even followed when I was smart.

I guess the only thing that I can say is thank you for the years of loyalty, advice, tutoring, kissed boo-boos, changed diapers, hot meals, clean clothes, and a shoulder to cry on, and for providing tolerance, patience, knowledge, and love—as well as being the greatest mother anyone could ever ask for. I love you.

Thanks, Mom!

Just Do It

HOWIE MANDEL

Comedian

I call my mother every day. We didn't always have that kind of relationship. When I lived in the same house, I could just go in the other room and say hello. Since I've moved away from Canada to another country—California—the phone has become the best tool for communication.

My perspective on my mother has changed immensely. I was sure she was a lot taller when I was younger. I'm always fascinated by how short she is. In my eyes, she was this giant of a woman at five feet two inches. I still think of my mom as larger than life, but now when she comes to visit, I stand her on the ottoman.

I've always had a great admiration and respect for my mother. Now that I'm a father of three kids, I'm in awe of the responsibility of parenting and the perspective it gives you on life. I used to think she was overprotective and much more worried than she ever had to be. Mom is still concerned if I've eaten enough and if I'm wearing a jacket. When she wants me to take a sweater along, I still do. It turns out she's a fraction of how protective and worrisome I have become as a parent. I've taken it to a new realm— but it's also a different world now.

We couldn't get much closer than we are. I've lived away from her for twenty-three years and I have not missed a day of talking to her at least once. I see her every few weeks. She travels on the road with me—she chooses the places she wants to go. It's always the ones with the best shopping and the nicest climates. She doesn't join me in Iowa, but she has visited me in Hawaii.

She's always had a great perspective on life—I don't know where she gets it from. I hope to have inherited a certain percentage of it. She had this philosophy far before Nike—and that was "Just Do It." I was thrown out of high school and I never finished, but she was always a champion of whatever I did. Her main credo in life was "As long as you're happy." So when I found the stage and acting, I had no bigger supporter than my parents.

They sat in audiences with so much pride. Certainly my greatest and number one press agents have always been my parents. I have a lot of friends and people in this business—especially comedians—whose parents have not been so thrilled with this choice, but my parents were not like that at all.

You always remember the first little nursery rhyme or philosophy that your mom has given you. The first saying I remember my mom uttering to me, and I think I could barely walk at the time, was:

Jean, Jean made a machine.
Joe, Joe, made it go.
Art, Art blew a fart
And blew the whole machine apart.

That was the first song, the first poem, the first bit of philosophy in my life. I think that those words are the ones I live by and are the ones that make me who I am today. I have nobody to thank more than my mother for that.

My mother has a terrific sense of humor and she's very up with what's going on in the world of entertainment and politics. She spent the majority of her life working—she was one of the top real estate salespeople in Canada. I can talk to her about anything and have an open, adult conversation. There is no feeling we have about each other that we don't share. All the love I could possibly feel has been told to her in person.

The one thing I can't get from my mother is criticism. I cannot do anything wrong. I can't go to her for an honest critique or an objective view of a performance.

I can say to her, "Mom, everybody stood up and left."

She'll say, "That's because you were so terrific, they couldn't take it anymore."

"What do you mean? It didn't go well. They left!"

"No. They just felt you were ruining it for them. If they stayed they wouldn't see anything the rest of their life that would reach that level."

There's nothing that I can do in her eyes that could be a negative. The glass has always been half full. It's always been about taking the path that would make you the happiest. She's taught me that you find success when you find something in life that you can't wait to wake up and try to do, whether it's being a parent, chasing a career, or enjoying the relationships of the people you surround yourself with. I was lucky enough to have that happen to me. Success has never been about the amount of money I've made or about the number of television appearances I've done. To me, success was finding something that made me happy—just like my mother said—and hopefully, that's what I will pass on to my children.

Ultimately you learn as you grow up, your mother means everything to you and she *is* you. Our mothers are always with us and always a part of us. I happen to be one of the lucky ones who doesn't think of that as a negative.

Better Difficult Than Dull

HARRY SMITH

Broadcast Journalist

My mother is very, very religious and has absolute faith in God—it is part of her real core. She has one of those beliefs that would go so far as to say, "God would never give you a challenge that you can't handle." She's ninety-two now, and two years ago she was not in great health and we really thought we were going to lose her. I brought her home from the hospital and I stayed with her for several days afterward. On the second day, she wanted a bath. I got out the chair that you sit in the tub with and my mother disrobed in front of me. At that time she was ninety years old, and when she took her clothes off I saw what ninety years of a really hard life had done to her body—not the least of which was the radical mastectomy that had left this cave on the left side of her torso when she was diagnosed with breast cancer in the mid-1970s. As I washed her back, the tears just streamed down my face. I was so thankful for the opportunity to be of some service to her in that way. You would never know how difficult life has been for her from her disposition, but as she was there in front of me, I knew everything.

Her attitude has always been "better difficult than dull." She grew up really poor and part of a huge family where she was one of twelve children. Her father walked out on her family and she seemed to always know how to take care of herself. She's just very, very gutsy. In 1996, she had quadruple bypass surgery. When the doctors examined her they told her she had the constitution of a sixty-year-old. She fought back like crazy. She's not without her down days, but she really is a fighter. She's fiercely independent.

As the youngest of eight, I was really lucky. My oldest brothers and sisters grew up during the Depression. By the time I came along in 1951 my oldest sister was married, my oldest brother was soon to be married, and a number of the kids were out of the house already. Talk about a surprise! My mother was forty years old and no one who was forty in 1951 was having babies. The closest brother in age to me was six years older. It was interesting to be part of this gigantic family, but I got more time with my mother than any of my siblings had. To my mother I wasn't God's gift, I was a gift from God.

She had worked so hard and was so busy raising all of those children that when I came along, I think she was able to give me more nurturing time. My father worked two jobs most of his life—he was a milkman and a part-time cop. We never wanted for anything, but there were no luxuries. My mother's generosity of spirit was stunning. When she turned eighty-five we threw a special birthday party that my wife and I organized with all the children and their spouses. I told my siblings, all you have to do is stand up and tell a story about the good old days. My oldest brother, Sam, got up and told this story about when they were living in this tiny house with four children during the Depression. My mother would ask my father for extra pennies every Friday. The reason she asked is because if she had them, she could buy extra flour and she could bake more bread, because the homeless people would come to the back of their teeny-tiny house looking for food, and she always felt compelled to help. My family had nothing, but even though they had so little, she felt they still needed to give something.

I don't think we really, really got close until I got older. As a young adult I encountered some difficult times. I was having a tough go of it. My father had died and things weren't going great for me in my career or my personal life. She was by herself and I was very much by myself in Denver, where I was trying to get my career in broadcasting going. We ended up communicating by mail and telephone. We shared books. With the couple of cents I had, I took her to Europe and we visited our relatives in Holland, where we went looking for family roots. The trip wound up launching this whole career of senior travel for her—she's been to Israel, Hawaii, and back to Europe again. She's done so many things that I don't think she would have done had things turned out differently. She was well into her seventies when she got on skis for the first time. She spent her entire adult life as a mom/spouse, and now she was on her own for the first time. We developed a closeness that hasn't changed since.

My mother has an amazing gift of appreciation for the smallest things. When I talk to her on the phone, we talk about the weather a lot because it has everything to do with whether or not her back door can be opened or a window can let in a fresh breeze. We talk about what kinds of birds are on the birdfeeder in the backyard and did I see a finch today? I'll tell her that I was in Central Park and saw a red-tailed hawk. She could listen to that forever. We laugh a lot.

She has a little patio outside her house in Lansing, Illinois, and after coming home from the hospital two years ago she ordered patio furniture for the first time in her life because it would have never occurred to her before that to just sit outside. If you were going outside, you were going to work out there. She thought, if I can't work like I want to, I'll sit with my plants.

My mother has always been a safe place to land for me. The thing that we learned about each other after my father died was that whatever our differences were, whatever things that were going on in my life that she might not have appreciated, she really was going to love me no matter what. The unconditional love that you sense as a child you really come to believe in as an adult.

A Valuable Lesson

DEBORAH ROBERTS

Broadcast Journalist

My relationship with my mother has gotten more complicated as we've gotten older. When I was growing up, she and I were very close—not because we always saw eye to eye, but simply because we had a warm, loving relationship. I was a shy, emotional child and I felt that she went out of the way to protect my feelings whenever I felt insecure. As I have grown older, however, and I started to broaden my horizons in my career—working in different places, different states, and learning so much more about the world—our relationship has become a little more complex. My mother is a very traditional, small-town person, so she doesn't always relate to the kinds of things that either interest me or consume me because of my career.

Becoming a mother myself changed everything dramatically for me. It led me to feel so much more respect and admiration for my mother and her years of struggle as a stay-at-home mom who pushed her identity to the background while raising nine children. I also gained a deeper understanding of her frustrations over the years, because suddenly I'm thrust into this role of shaping a life and all the fallout that comes from having children. I remember times when my mother was short-tempered or not as patient as I wish she had been. I grew up in the South, where the attitude really was "Spare the rod, spoil the child." I definitely got my share of spankings, or "whippings" as we called them in Georgia. There were incidents where I didn't think my mom was really very fair to me during childhood disputes, but now I sort of get where she was coming from. It's difficult to reason with a child. My mother, who dropped out of high school to help support her family, wasn't the beneficiary of an education like I was, so she was really going on her instinct.

Now we laugh and share baby stories. The other night I was talking to her about how my new baby boy wakes up through the night. She shared stories about me doing the very same thing and told me about a talk show she had discovered all because she was up with me during the wee hours of the morning. She loves to tell those kinds of stories. Instead of offering unsolicited advice during this period of being a new mother, she shares her spirit of tenacity, of how this, too, shall pass. She doesn't tell me what to do but she gives me this feeling that it will be fine, and that's very comforting. If I were to ask her, she would then offer, "Well, in my day we did *this*." Mostly, she just listens.

My mother's mother died when she was a baby, and she was raised by a very stern grandmother, so her attitude throughout life is that you just suck it in and do it. There isn't a whole lot of sharing of complaints—in her time it was a luxury to complain about difficulties. Her philosophy has always been that you just get through things and just do it. It's more about going on and doing what you have to do, and in some ways that attitude has made me stronger.

My parents didn't always get along and they went through a lot of marital troubles. I think I was sort of judgmental—I always blamed my father if they were having a disagreement or I blamed my mother about other things. Of course, I see life as a lot more complex now that I have a husband and a family. I realize there are complications in relationships and my mother is a *woman*, not just my mother. She had desires, needs, and concerns that played into her marriage that I wasn't privy to. I now understand more about their troubles. Maybe some of them related to the way my mother was raised, and maybe she wasn't as emotional as my father wanted her to be.

My mother was, for the most part, the disciplinarian because she was home with the kids all day. It was the classic, traditional marriage. My father worked all day and came home late. We didn't see him as much except on the weekends, so he was absent from the world of punishment and childhood turmoil.

A few years ago, we lost my brother, who was thirty-nine. Both of my parents were torn up over the loss, but my dad was more demonstrative with his emotions. My husband first pointed it out to me. It was something I never thought much about while growing up. I guess I didn't see my parents as people, just as Mom and Dad. Maybe that played into some of their difficulties over the years. The experience drew me closer to both of them. Suddenly I began to understand them as two complex people trying to deal with their own background and upbringing.

My mother doesn't really open up, and that's where the complexities have entered our relationship, because I am a person who likes to delve into issues, feelings, and emotions, and my mother isn't. Because I have attempted to tap into her feelings on certain things and I don't really get very far, that's made it hard. One of my sisters counseled me when I was deeply frustrated about a conversation I had with my mother. She said to me, "You have to stop wanting Mom to be who you want her to be and accept her for who she is."

I would love to have my parents travel more and come visit us more. The fact is they don't like to fly, and nowadays with the security concerns, it makes them terribly nervous. There are things that I want to do with my mother that she doesn't necessarily want to do. There were times when I wanted to buy her fancy new outfits. I'd say, "This is going to look great on you, Mom!" But she never wears them—things wind up in the back of her closet. I wanted her to do these things, but what I realized is that I wanted her to be the mother I wanted her to be. Realizing I had to accept and love her for who she is has had a profound impact on me.

In spite of these complexities, I have inherited many wonderful traits from her. My work ethic came from my mother—during my teen years she was always adamant about how important it was to get up early and chase that opportunity. When we were looking for summer jobs, my mother would hound us to go and check out any possibility around town. No job was too small or demeaning. Because she grew up in the traditional South, the notion of a career wasn't in her grasp. It wasn't something she could pass on to me, but it was certainly something she wanted for me. She wanted her girls to be strong and not to have to depend on a man, and that had a lot to do with my tenacity and my pursuit of my goals.

My mother is a very religious person and many of her feelings about life are based on spiritual principles. She believes you are obliged to do what you can. She always reached out to people who were hurting and down on their luck, and would give a homeless man something to eat over the backyard fence. I thought it was strange then, but her feeling was everyone is God's child. I've adopted those principles over the years and now very much appreciate her sense of compassion and her incredibly good heart.

The greatest lesson my mother has taught me that has stayed with me over the years is to care about your fellow man. You can achieve your goals but you still have to find a way to reach out to others. I'm in a career where it's very competitive, but because of my mother I think I still have a sense of fairness. Even though I'm out chasing stories, trying to elbow other people to get them, I know I can still be a good person. My mother is a very gentle spirit and has not spoken up a lot in her life, but I heard her loud and clear. I have come to treasure her. I love you, Mom.

Live & Learn

DAISY FUENTES

Actress

My mom had me when she was very young—she had just turned nineteen—so she didn't get to experience a whole lot in life. I have lived so much because of my career that sometimes now the roles get reversed. But she is the glue that holds the family together.

As the years go on, I realize that she is very innocent. Her innocence is really a wonder to me—that she has been able to hold on to that in spite of all the things she's gone through in life. I see her as an innocent child almost—in a very sweet way because I've become street savvy as a result of the things we've been through. Even though she's experienced a lot—as far as leaving her native Cuba, going to Spain, and then going to the United States with us to escape political turmoil—she's still innocent in so many ways.

I was born in Cuba and lived in Spain until I was eight, and then we moved to New Jersey. It was very hard for me when I came to this country. I didn't know anything. I did not speak a word of the language and I didn't understand the culture and customs. My mom went to work right away in a factory, having to put her kids in day care. She couldn't see herself working in a factory all her life, so she put herself through school and learned computer skills, and now she's a computer programmer-analyst. She really struggled to better herself.

We don't talk about all the things she went through. I think she just went on instinct—which is probably why she doesn't have a whole lot to say about this. I don't think she knows how she did it. I don't think she's thought about it a whole lot and that's why she's been such a survivor. She's just always done what she had to do.

She brought all of my Spanish books from Spain when we came to this country. My mom realized I was going to be quite Americanized and she was not about to let me forget my roots. So on top of my English homework from school, she would teach me Spanish in her own Spanish classes a couple of times a week and even give me homework. I hated it at the time, but now I think it's amazing that she even thought of that and put everybody before her own needs.

My mother is a breast cancer survivor. When we went through her illness about fifteen years ago, we were so uneducated about the disease. She was only forty but she caught it very early. I remember her saying to me, "I went to my doctor and my doctor says I shouldn't worry about it, but I don't feel right." I said, "No, Mommy, if you don't feel right we have to go somewhere else." That whole experience and thinking about possibly losing her—I just couldn't fathom it. The whole family just did a complete turnaround. I remember how strong she was when she had the operation and how my dad, my sister, and I were hanging around the hospital in the street in New York City waiting for this operation to be over and trying to stay busy and not think about it. It was, like, "Let's go get a Coke. No, let's go look at this. Let's go look at that." It was so traumatizing and we walked around in circles trying not to think about what was going on. Fortunately, everything turned out great. She's been cancer-free since. She's been really good at staying on top of it. I think the experience scared the life *into* her. It made her think she had to enjoy life *now*.

I very much hope I share the love of life that she has. She is such a happy soul and she's got such a good heart. When I think of my mom, I think of someone who loves to dance, who likes to be with friends, who loves to hang out with her family, who loves to travel. She doesn't seem to let anything get her down.

My mom also doesn't think anything is impossible. When I got my first television job as a weather anchor in New York, I was still living at home and I got to work for the Spanish news channel. I'd never done television and I said to her, "How can I do live television?" And she said, "Of course you can do it. Go do it!" I remember halfway through it thinking, "I'd really love that MTV job. That is where I should be working. I'm too young to be in the news." And she said, "You should send them a tape." I said, "Mom, I don't even have an agent—that's not how you do things." She said, "No, seriously. Get your friends at the network to make a tape, then send it. Do it!" She was such a pain in the ass about it that I finally did it, and that's how I got my MTV job. She doesn't think about the reasons why you can't do something—and that's part of her innocence. She just always thinks you can do it. She has taught me not to think about things too much, and if there's something I want, to go for it.

She took up painting a few years ago and she's wonderful at it. The paintings are all over the house and she's given some to me and some to her friends. Once in a while she stops and I have to remind her how good she is. One day I'd like to do a gallery showing for her as a fund-raiser. She's great. I'm very proud that she just took this up late in life because it was something that she thought she'd enjoy. She has inspired me to take it up, too.

I travel a lot for my job and now she sometimes comes along for the fun of it. One of our favorite trips was when we went to Monte Carlo for the World Music Awards. To be able to take my mom on a trip like that was so fabulous. It was like having a girlfriend with me and I forgot she was my mom half the time. When we were getting dressed to go out, I'd say, "What do you mean you can't wear that?" Then I'd think, "No, she can't. She's my mom!"

She and my dad live in Miami now and I visit a lot. I'm kind of her stylist. Every time I go, I always have to straighten her hair and give her a French manicure. Obviously, she does just fine when I'm not there, but she acts like it's been months. She loves it. I'm proud of how good she looks.

My mother has taught me that you've just got to live your life and to take in the everyday experiences. I've never been very book smart. She always tried to get me to study and go to school, but I've never been very good with that. I dropped out of college. Just knowing she got married so young and didn't really get to experience a lot has made me really determined to learn as much about the world as I can. She always says, "You've got a great opportunity to experience life, so you should do it." Thanks to her, I have. I don't tell her often enough, but I love her.

A Tree Grows in Memphis

DANA BUCHMAN

Designer

My mother took great joy in going against the crowd and being a bit of a provocateur. Growing up in Memphis, we were the only Democrats in the Republican part of town and she just loved that. During the Nixon-Kennedy campaign, Richard Nixon drove by our school when I was ten. I said, "Annie, I saw Richard Nixon today!" And she said, "Who cares? We're Democrats."

She always told me you don't have to follow the crowd and do what other people do.

There was an irreverence about her that, I think, had a huge influence on the type of people her children became. In high school I became interested in fashion and I had a very faint rebellious streak. There was a period where I'd go barefoot and wrap ribbons around my feet, which even though I'd get sent home from school for doing it, she thought it was just fine. During the time of Mary Quant body paint, I'd paint colors all over my legs and get sent home for that, too. She thought that was no problem.

I called her Momma early on, but I guess because my sister Leslie, who is ten years older, started calling her Annie, I did, too. Annie's greatest pleasure was to be at home—she gardened and read a lot. She loved to sit on the porch and talk to me and see what was going on in my life. Annie was tall and she always taught my sister and me to stand up straight and go ahead and be tall. I think it bothered her in her day. She felt too tall, but the theory that she passed on to us was don't try to hide it—be glad about who you are.

My mother was not a big acquirer of things. We didn't buy a lot. There was plenty but I didn't have tons and tons of clothes. You'd make do. To use something to wear it out was a virtue. I have had a little of that but it's wearing off living in New York. She believed in the arts, literature, relationships, and ideas. My father and she would have dinner parties. She wasn't always redoing the bathroom and yet she did take great pleasure in her house and how it looked. It was simple but very elegant. She was incredibly warm but she wasn't a sentimental-type mom at all. She'd send my daughters funny little things but forget birthdays—that was kind of her thing about being an iconoclast, too. She thought you didn't have to celebrate birthdays. As far as she was concerned, Mother's Day was created by Hallmark—you should honor your mother every day. I named one of my daughters, Annie Rose, after her. My other daughter, Charlotte, is named after my husband's aunt. In the South people always name children after someone, and I married a Jewish man whose family never names anyone after anyone still alive. When Tom and I had our daughter, my mother became Big Annie. Of course Annie was also named after her mother's sister, Rose.

We were a very close family. My father was part owner of a steel fabricating plant and started work at seven o'clock in the morning, so we always had breakfast at six. Annie would get up and bring breakfast upstairs to their bedroom and all the children were invited in to eat breakfast off the tray. If you missed it, you were on your own. It was a great time—we were half asleep munching on whatever Annie had fixed.

When I was thirteen, she took my brother and me to Europe. We bought a VW van in Amsterdam and drove through France and Switzerland and down to the bottom of Italy and took a ferry to Greece and met my sister in Turkey, who was there working for the state department. Jim, who was sixteen, would drive and I would read the map and we'd put Annie in the back because she was such a backseat driver. We played double solitaire at night and got into big fights—we were a very competitive group. The three of us visited cathedrals and museums and had picnics. It was really lovely. It wasn't a fancy trip, and later when I traveled for business, I saw a completely different Europe.

Annie was always so supportive. My brother is a sculptor and she thought that was great. I studied English and when I switched to fashion, she thought that was great. Her children didn't exist to be her status symbols—she took great pleasure in hearing which way we were going with ourselves. Her appreciation of art and literature was a great influence on us. She was always reading. Once a week we'd go to the library and she made us read. "Why don't you read a book? Read, Dana. Just read," she'd say, just sort of badgering me. Now I love reading—it's a major part of my life today. It's funny, something about her drove me to want to achieve, but I don't feel as if I was pushed.

We always wrote long letters to each other while I was in college at Brown. She'd write using carbon paper so sometimes the carbon paper would be in backward. I'd get the front and back of my letter and my sister's letter, and Leslie wouldn't get one. While I was away at college Annie decided to go back and get her master's degree in English at what is now called the University of Memphis. We'd coach her on writing her papers from college. She'd read me the paper or send it to me and I'd make corrections and we'd get in fights—"What do you mean, Dana? I think it's very clear!"

Our relationship changed for the first time when I came home from college because all of a sudden I was somewhat autonomous. It changed again when my father died in 1981. Annie would never join a support group or anything like that. She looked for solace in reading. She had some really good friends and gardened and went about making up for this loss. It was a wonderful marriage, so it was a huge loss to her. She just made it work.

She was much more available after my father died, and she traveled with me on my frequent flyer miles. Once she flew to Hong Kong just to be there for a couple of days. She wasn't really interested in sightseeing in those days, she was just interested in being with me, so we'd have the plane ride over and have meals together. She was a great traveler—she so enjoyed the luxuries we had. At the time I had 600,000 miles on Pan Am, so we flew first class everywhere, which I had never done growing up. In those days Pan Am would give you caviar and sirloin, and she just loved it and wasn't above saying how much fun it all was. She would make me look at things with such pleasure because she took such joy in them.

She was a huge influence on my life because she always made me feel smart and beautiful and loved. I always felt I could go home, and now that it's not there, I still have the qualities within me. If there was a disappointment she would empathize with me but it would be like, "Just hold your shoulders up," or, "It's their loss." She was an advocate for her children and let us know it. There was never any nagging. The only thing that bothered her about me was that I didn't carry a purse.

She went with me to the fashion shows I did around the country. Annie didn't like wide-legged pants. I'd have to make her ones with slim legs—that was her look. She was a beautiful woman. She loved wearing my clothes, but if she didn't like something, she'd be honest. She'd say, "Why are you making those old, wide-legged pants?" I'd say, "Well, Annie, some people like them."

Nothing really changed between us when I became a mother. She was a really attentive, careful grandmother and mother-in-law—careful not to intrude. She waited a couple of days after my daughter was born to meet Charlotte, my oldest, and stayed one day. She was very careful not to impose but I was ecstatic having her there. My daughters, who are both teenagers now, realize how much my mother meant to me, so they have absorbed that. I talk a lot about her and about when I was growing up. When you have children, things that happened in your own childhood spring back to life.

We talked on the phone every day. She'd tell me how the tomatoes were growing in Memphis, how the dog was doing, and also share more important things, like how she was feeling. She loved hearing about my life and what was going on and who I met. One thing that was different between us was she liked the phone to ring. She was always like, "Who could that *be?*" whereas with me it's, "*Who* could that be?"

My mother had been sort of declining around the time of her death in 1994. She had fallen. She loved the house we grew up in, which she and my father had built. My grandmother, who lived next door, gave them a couple of acres of what was then a cow pasture, which later became the center of suburban Memphis. They built this house that was just beautiful—it was small but elegant and lovely. She loved it and didn't want to leave. She had beautiful, beautiful gardens. I was trying to talk her into having someone come in and stay with her occasionally and she'd say, "No way!"

We spoke on a Friday and she finally said, "Okay, I'll do that." My sister had driven over to pick her up for a weekend visit because she felt Annie needed a little boost. They were driving out and my sister remembers Annie looked back at the house as if she were saying good-bye. She died in the car on the way to my sister's house—she just fell asleep. It was very poetic. When we went down for the funeral, I'd never seen the garden looking more magnificent. She had these amazing moon trees in full bloom with these big, huge floaty flowers. The house looked lovely—everything was gleaming and shiny. It was a beautiful tribute to her.

Annie just loved being alive. She made me look at things with new pleasure because she took such joy in them. She took such relish in everyday things—the beauty of her flowers, the smell of her black coffee, the smell of trees. She lived in the moment. The other day I was rushing to work and I thought, wait a minute— look up at the sky. It made me think of her and smile.

I wish she could be here and see my life now. She would have loved the girls as teenagers. My daughter Annie Rose has picked up a little on Big Annie's way of thinking. She's in ninth grade and all the kids in her class are obsessed with doing things that will look good on their record, and she said to me recently, "What are we doing? We're doing all these things *just* so we get into college. Then we're going to be doing stuff *just* so we get a job. When do you start living?" Listening to her, I knew that it was Annie's influence through me that was coming through—it's just what Annie would have thought.

Steel Magnolias

NANCY GRACE

Television Anchor
and
Former Prosecutor

One of my first and most vivid memories took place when I was about three years old, sitting cross-legged in pine straw at the base of a fat old pine tree. I looked up into the heat of a summer day in Georgia and noticed my mother picking her way toward me, unspeaking. She continued stepping forward, placing each foot carefully before the other and slowly, simultaneously, raised a sharp gardener's hoe over her right shoulder like a spear. Never considering I was in harm's way, neither of us uttered a sound when she pulled back and then plunged the hoe forward straight toward me. It landed in the dirt with a thud and I turned to see she had taken off the head of a rattlesnake coiled up behind me. She dropped down, scooped me up, and took me inside.

My family lived in farmland with nothing but tall pine trees, red dirt roads, and soybean fields as far as the eye could see. It was a hard-working farming area, and when it dawned on me how my parents struggled to take care of us all, there was no way I could bear to disappoint them. I recall my mom never once raised her voice to me in all those years, a simple pursing of her lips always seemed to do the trick!

My mother, Elizabeth, played cello in the Georgia Symphony in her younger days. I remember listening to her practice piano late into the night as we children fell asleep. Even now, she plays a huge organ every Sunday at the little white-board Methodist church where we grew up. I distinctly remember my mother sewing fast and furious, making our Easter Sunday clothes from bolts of cloth. It was only years later that it dawned on me that my sister and I always had the same dress . . . she'd make both of our outfits from a single bolt! But oh, how we loved them at the time and oh, how beautiful we thought those outfits were. Looking back on it, I think they were even more beautiful because she made them. My mother schooled me in everything from canning your own green beans and apple jelly, to practicing public speaking starting at age nine in our local 4-H club. She would practice and practice with me for the next seven years. Believe me, in years to come it came in handy when I had to look a jury in the eye and argue a murder, a rape, or a child molestation case to its verdict.

The two of them, my mom and dad, steered the three of us through the ups and downs of life, but a defining moment came when I was in undergraduate school, studying to become an English professor, and my wedding date was not far away. I received a horrible phone call informing me my fiancé had been killed in a horrible act of random violence, a mugging, a murder. During the weeks and months that followed, she stood by me, consoled me, and led me through what then seemed to be a never-ending, dark tunnel. Instead of the heartbreak breaking me, my parents helped me emerge from that dark time even stronger.

Not only did my parents see me through that turbulent time, but my mother stood by me during the next decade as I decided to enter law school and go on to become a felony prosecutor of violent crime in inner city Atlanta. She often traveled hours to sit in the courtroom while I tried cases—murder, theft, arson, you name it. We talked trial strategy and jury selection into the night, evaluating witnesses, judges, and defense attorneys.

She encouraged me to make a quantum leap from local prosecutor to television legal analyst when I joined Court TV. Even now, she never misses a single appearance. She especially loves the *Larry King Live* shows, and I always call her afterwards to either celebrate a great night or gnash through whatever the opposition had to say! She's my biggest fan and toughest critic, never sparing the truth, whether it's about my legal analysis, my demeanor on air, or even my hair and makeup. And she still corrects me if I interrupt on-air!

As this goes to press, I think of her. She has a glow from the inside out that lights up a room and makes everyone feel warmer but more important; she is one of those wonderful, never-say-die individuals who believe we each have been blessed with everything we could possibly need or want, we have only to summon it up from inside. I so hope some of her radiance somehow rubbed off on me. Mother, I love you so.

Making the Grade

ROBIN ROBERTS

Broadcast Journalist

The things that used to upset me about my mother as a child, I find myself praising as an adult. She held to her values. Now that I'm in television I have to speak proper English, but growing up in Mississippi, I wanted to be lazy and talk like my friends. I thought I was being good leaving a note telling her when I went to play at someone's house, but when I came home it would be corrected in red ink. I thought, "Let me be a kid!"

My mom was an elementary-school teacher and worked mainly as a substitute. She even taught when we were living in Turkey. My dad, who was in the Air Force, was stationed there. She would bring her Turkish students home and it was wonderful to be around them. We didn't live on a military base, we lived in an apartment with Turkish families. My mother thought, "Why do you want to live in a foreign country on an American base? That makes no sense." Our lives were real educations. It was fun, everything was an adventure.

My mother was the first in her family to get a college degree— she went to Howard University, where she met my father. Like so many mothers of her generation she put her life on hold as soon as she got married—my dad and the children became the focus. Once we were all out of the house (I was the youngest of four), she was appointed to the state board of education of Mississippi, of which she later became the chair. My mom was on the board of directors of the Federal Reserve Bank of Atlanta, New Orleans branch. She did her job as a mom and then it was like, "Okay, my turn." She even told my dad that. She moved thirty-some-odd times for his job—he was a Tuskegee Airman. He retired as a full colonel in 1975 after having been in the service for thirty years. I loved how when we were out on our own she stepped up and said it was her turn. It's wonderful to see her do the kinds of things I knew she wanted to do when she was younger but put her family first.

We weren't always close. With mothers and daughters it's wonderful but it's also difficult at times. We always loved each other and there were always defined roles—she was the mother and I was the daughter. There was no gray area there and sometimes I didn't like her authority. I didn't always want to go to church on Sunday but it was like, "No, you're going." But now it's like a reflex for me. Things like that are so much a fabric of who you are as an adult, but as a child that's certainly not the case. During high school our relationship was very strained. I played basketball and didn't want my mom and dad to come to the games. I never let them come and see me play. In college, it got a little bit better. I remember my mom first dropping me off at the dorm. She told me later it was all that she could do not to turn around and come and get me a couple of days later because she missed me so much. Had she come back, I would have gotten into the car and gone home. I'm so glad she didn't. She gave me roots but also pushed me out of the nest.

It wasn't until I became a full-fledged adult working and making minimum wage in my first job—I was a weekend sports anchor making $5.50 an hour working thirty hours a week—that we began to develop a close relationship. Later I was offered a full-time position in news making $15,000 a year. My mom was very supportive when I decided to pass it up. When other people said

I should take the full-time position she said, "No, Robin wants to do sports. If that's what she wants to do, her father and I will continue to help." And she did. Even when she knew it was going to be difficult to be a woman in sports, she and my father never wavered in their support.

As she has gotten older, it's beautiful how the relationship has evolved. I kick myself sometimes and ask why I wasted so much time. I so admire my mother's goodness. She has a wonderful laugh. I never, ever have heard my mother use profanity. She has such a good heart. She is a Christian and very church-minded, but she doesn't go around spouting scripture. But when you're around her, you can feel her goodness and you want to emulate it. She can see the good not only in her children and her family, but in everyone. You really have to do something bad to get under my mom's skin. She calls me almost every single time I go off the air and she's always excited. I always think, how can she be excited to hear my voice when we spoke less than twenty-four hours ago? You would have thought we hadn't spoken in years. I love that excitement in her voice.

My friends sometimes call me "Pollyanna," so I think I have the same kind of "I want to save the world" qualities that my mother has. She has taught me not to be skeptical of people and to give them a chance, which is difficult in this business, where we are skeptical by nature. I'm also grateful that I learned from her to rely on my faith. I'm so appreciative that she has lived her life like that.

She didn't force it on any of her children, but as I get older I really draw upon it, especially in unsettling times like the ones we live in and especially being in the media and knowing what I know about what's going on in the world. I'm grateful that I've adopted from her the idea that real strength lies in your faith. Because I'm now in the news media and not so much in sports, she worries. She does that with all her children, but especially me, because I'm the only one who is unmarried. She's more protective of me than of my older siblings. When I came up to ESPN in the mid-1980s for an interview, my flight was delayed and all these things were going wrong. I walked into this Motel 6 at two in the morning and the guy behind the desk gave me this look and said, "Call your mother." Of course, I did.

She has been invaluable to me in helping me achieve my goals. She gave me the courage to do something different and always told me I could come back home. I remember coming home from a career day in the sixth grade. I came in and said, "I'm going to be a teacher and teach physical education and be a coach because that's the only way as a girl that I can be involved in sports." She's like, "No, you're not. You're totally selling out and thinking that's the only thing you could do. Go back outside and find something else." I thought she'd be excited but she knew me so well. She told me, don't look at what people are doing, look outside of that and figure out what it is that is going to make you happiest. I really wanted to be a professional athlete but didn't have the ability. I took up bowling—I wanted to be a bowling champion. She'd take me all around the state. In high school I realized that I wasn't going to be a professional athlete, and I have an older sister, Sally-Ann, who was in broadcasting as a news anchor–reporter in New Orleans. I was looking to her, and my mother was the one who encouraged me. She wanted me to open up my thinking—not to open up a magazine or look at television and say, "I don't see someone who looks like me, so I can't do this." That wasn't going to fly with her.

I always felt her support—it was so unconditional. I was a black woman in the Deep South who wanted to do sports on television. Sure, that's going to happen, I'd think. But she never let me use gender or race as an excuse. She'd say, "If you're not going to get it, it's because you're not good enough, it's not because you're black or because you're a woman. You've got to work for it like everybody else." I loved that she never allowed any of us to use race as a crutch.

My mother used to say something before I left the house: "You know right from wrong." Because of my mother and my father, I did know right from wrong and it helped me make decisions. Just that simple phrase would steer me back on course. When my friends would do something that really wasn't right and I knew it, I'd think, "Why did she say that to me? I do know right from wrong and I can't do this." I loved that she never backed down. Sometimes I think parents now are intimidated by their children—they want them to like them. My momma didn't care if we liked her or not. Some of my friends had younger mothers— my mom was older when she had me. I would think, "Gosh, that mom is so hip. I wish my mother could be like that." It's amazing that I would ever think that, because now I know in my heart, I wouldn't trade her for anyone else in the world.

A Mixed Blessing

EMME

**Vocal Women's
Advocate,
Author,
Clothing Designer,
Wife,
and Mom**

As a little girl, I would often play in my mother's closet. I was mesmerized by her room and all the exotic things in it. I loved the smell of her perfume, Joy by Jean Patou. I remember how she would hold the big glass bottle upside down before removing its very heavy top. Then, with her perfectly manicured fingertips in this ultra-feminine shade of pale pink polish, she'd take the top and put it behind her ears. I remember that so clearly.

One of my mom's strongest qualities was putting people at ease no matter where they came from. She had been exposed to a great deal in her life. Her father was a geologist and she was born in Trinidad, grew up in Florence, Italy, and Egypt, and went to school in Switzerland. She always encouraged me to think outside the box. When we traveled to different countries and I saw her eating eel in Italy or trying different wines, I saw that it was okay to be different or have different ideas. I really, really appreciate that kind of mom.

I remember how influenced I was by all the little social graces that she knew, like how to set a table. She didn't have a lot of money, because when she divorced my father, her father, my grandfather, didn't want to help her because he had a problem with divorce. She just always managed to make everything very, very fun. She would light candles for us at dinner and teach me how to use the three forks, two knives, three spoons, and many different glasses. I would not always know what to do, but she would always be patient.

She always included me in dinner parties at the house and she'd show me what she was doing, saying, "Now *this* is how you throw a party." Everything was always laid out nicely so everyone could have a good time. She used to entertain barefoot—she always painted her toenails red and she had the most beautiful, tanned toes. I do the same thing now, but my feet aren't nearly as pretty. She had beautiful clothes that were comfortable and easy but always very refined and kind of sexy. Whenever she would open the front door to a party she was having, it must have looked as if the whole world was opening up right before that guest. Her aura twinkled. I know now that when I entertain, I get so much joy out of having people come to the house, whether it's for pizza or when we get all dressed up. That's when I bring out the good silver and do a full dinner party with really expensive wine and great cheeses. I learned from my mother that there is nothing better than breaking bread with friends. I hope that when people walk into my house they get a sense of calm and feel peaceful, and they also have a sense that there's a little bit of mystery about what is going to unfold for the evening.

As a budding teenager getting my footing in life, I was living in Saudi Arabia and I got turned on to athletics by a teacher. It was this great fun thing for my mom. I don't think she really ever exercised. She'd laugh and say, "I can't believe you're getting so muscular." I remember I used to give her a playful punch on the arm and she'd look at me and say, "I swear to you, if you do that again, I'm going to fall over." I was different than her now—I was becoming more "me." She decided she'd try exercising and she asked me to show her how to run on the track. She ran like a bird! It was really, really sweet.

My mother died when I was sixteen. She was diagnosed with this horrendous form of cancer that probably originated as breast cancer and spread throughout her entire body. She did not like going to the doctor, so she didn't. She faced her situation with a smile on her face. She became ill when I was about thirteen. We were living in Saudi Arabia and the doctors there were good for what they were, but the technology wasn't as advanced as it was in the United States. As the months went by, she got sicker and sicker, and being a kid, I wanted my mom back—to come to my events and get back into my life. The times that I would spend with her, I was focused on helping her, which was a very different role for me at that age.

When she finally announced to the family that she did have cancer, she told my brother, sister, and me that she and my stepfather were going to have to go back to the States to get her care. We would have to stay in Saudi Arabia with friends. It was very frightening. She never came back. Her battle was over.

I have made a very big commitment to speak out about body image and diversity because my mom had gone through so many diets and spent so much of her life battling her body. I think I'm standing up for her and her generation. My mother's friends were always talking about liberation and I couldn't stand the fact that my stepfather didn't walk the walk and talk the talk. I want to get done what she couldn't get done for herself, but I'm doing it on a grander scale. I am walking the walk and talking the talk. I'm doing what my mom didn't get a chance to do, and that is being a little fearless and dealing with the consequences after you do what your gut is telling you to do. Life is short—what are you going to do with it? Are you going to just hang out? Are you going to say,

"Would have, could have, should have?" I hate those three expressions. It's not a daily thing I think about, but I want to make a difference in this world.

She had such a positive outlook and she knew how to get the nectar out of life. Now I don't just wear a smile for a smile's sake. I took a page out of her book and replaced it with my own. If I'm angry about something, I'm angry and I'm going to talk about it, but I don't let it keep me down. She once told me, "You have a fifty percent chance of thinking positively and a fifty percent chance of thinking negatively. Why don't you take the positive route? You're not in denial. You know what's going on, but at least you'll have a better ride through the bumpy parts."

I use what my mom did with me to give my baby daughter, Toby, a chance to express herself. There are little things that come up. Sometimes I think, "Oh wow, I'm doing this differently than she did" or, "I'm doing this the very same way." There's a part of me that's now able to forgive my mother for leaving me in the wings of life and not being there to support me and listen and talk to me about the things that matter, like a first love. I wish I had my mom here so I could talk to her about all the things I'm going through now.

Toby has all these different features—she looks like my mother's mother. Sometimes I look at her and think, "Wouldn't it be a blessing if my mom could see her." I think about how old she would be now, and then I cry—I believe you have to allow yourself to cry. They are tears of healing. There was a time when I got very angry and thought, "How dare you not be around for this, of all things. How could you not be around?" But I also have this wonderful thought that I'm bringing my mother's life forward. Even though she's not present, I sometimes smell my mother's perfume in Toby's room. I'll hear my mother calling out my name in the middle of the night and I'll jump out of bed. I'll be walking to Toby's room and pass through this feeling of *something*. I wouldn't have been thinking of her at that moment, but then I get the sense that she's there. I know in my heart she's right next to me, and because she loved me so much, she's never too far away. It's a blessing that I had the kind of mom that I did. I'm very, very lucky.

The Long
Good-bye

LINDA DANO

Actress

When I started out in life growing up in California, my mother was always my friend—a good friend, a confidante. I don't know how she did it, but she set it up where I felt safe enough to share secrets. When I went on a date I'd come into their bedroom, where my father probably was pretending to be asleep, and my mother and I would talk about the date. I remember once a boy tried to go too far and I was so horrified by it—I was such a nice little Catholic girl—that it scared the pants off me. My mother's take on it—and this is why she was so brilliant—was, "Well, you know, sweetheart, boys will be boys. If he thought he was going to get somewhere with you, he was going to try. It doesn't mean that he's a bad person." She did this whole philosophical thing. I felt better about it and better about him. I had him painted as a pervert, but what she said made sense. She was very smart that way. She set it up like that—we were friends, but the rules in my house were very clear. I never broke any of them, I was sickeningly good. I always wanted to please my parents—"God forbid you don't like me"—and I haven't gone far from that. My mother could, in that environment, create this friendship and still be my mother.

Everything really changed when my parents came to New York eleven years ago. My father at that time was, I thought, just getting old and cranky, when in fact he had Alzheimer's, which I didn't learn until about four weeks after they arrived. I was his caregiver and out of all of the pain of having to watch him be tormented, I knew on some level I was saving my mother, which now I can comfort myself with. I had always said I wouldn't put either of my parents in a nursing home and suddenly I was forced to put my father in a nursing home. It just threw me into a tailspin—I had a very tough time with it. It was the first time I didn't really share with my mother about how I was feeling because I wanted to protect her from that.

As the years have gone on with us living together, it has been interesting. After you've left your home and your family and have gone on to make your own family and you make your own decisions, it's difficult when your mom comes to live with you and there are two women in one house. But we came through that. Now my mother, who is ninety-two, has been suffering from dementia, so she has really needed me. The sad part of all of this with the dementia is that there are moments where my mother doesn't know who I am. That just sends me back into that tailspin again. It's very, very hard. The roles have been completely reversed now. She's the child and I'm the grown-up.

I tend to her like a child because she's very childlike. I have help because my mother cannot be left alone. This past year my mother fell and broke her hip and pelvis, so this has been a very difficult year. I thought this was going to be the end, but thank God she has rallied. She's doing okay but the relationship is hard. When I lost my father, I was no longer "Daddy's little girl." With my mother and the place that she's at, I am now the grown-up and I don't care if you live to be eighty, no one wants to be the grown-up. I don't. I want to go home and have my mother tuck me into bed and bring me soup when I'm sick and tell me I'm going to be okay, and she can't do that. Now I'm it and I have to say, I don't like being it.

But I hold on to the good parts of what we have. My mother gave me lots of things—first and foremost a deep commitment to family. She gave me a secure home—a place that was safe. My mother taught me manners. She gave me style—my mother has great style and I get mine from her. She helped me to understand relationships with men. My mother and father both gave me the sense that I could do anything—I could be anyone I wanted to be. The support of that—the coming to every event whatever it was—was invaluable.

When I look back at the advice my mother gave, at the time I didn't think it was particularly profound. It wasn't eloquent—she never even graduated from high school. My mother nursed her mother in illness and had to quit school to do that. When my older brother, Jack, was very ill and had cancer and was dying, it was my mother and father who went and lived in a trailer right near where he lived and stayed all day to take care of him. That has been a role model for me. This commitment to family, God, church, and friends was very heavily instilled in me. I have never, ever lost sight of where I come from and how grateful I am to be here, because they didn't have anything. I always knew it wasn't about money or position, it was about being happy. In the work I do and watching actors come and go and become someone they really shouldn't become, I've never gone down that road because my foundation was so strong. People have asked me through the years about what I would do if my husband asked me to give up acting, and I've said if he wanted to go to Timbuktu and live in a tent, I'd probably have to go. I might not like it, but I'd have to go because my first commitment is to family—something I undoubtedly inherited from my mother.

My sadness is I can no longer go to my mother and have her listen and understand what I'm saying and share my emotion. I would love that because now it's all on my shoulders. Most of the time it's okay and I've accepted it and I'm thrilled to have some lucid moments. I spend a lot of time sitting in her room and watching TV with her, trying to connect, but there are moments where I feel very sad because on some level she has already left me. So now I'm Mom.

A
Campaigning
Mom

PAT SCHROEDER

**Former
Congresswoman**

My mother, Bernice Scott, should be made a saint for all she went through raising me to adulthood. She was born and raised in Nebraska. Her mother was four foot eight inches tall, so she thought she was a giant at five feet weighing ninety pounds. I weighed nine pounds at birth and was five foot seven by fifth grade. Mother had beautiful blonde hair, I had brown. She was sure the hospital had given her the wrong baby from the very beginning. That was just the beginning of the huge differences between us. Mother was always the model child, played with dolls, and had a degree in early childhood education. I always pushed the limits, played with airplanes, and got a pilot's license. Then I went to Harvard Law School. She was sure no one would marry me and she would never have grandchildren. When all that happened, she was thrilled. Then while my parents were on a trip to Asia, I announced for Congress. It was 1972, and people were shocked a mother of a two- and six-year-old would run for Congress. Remember the famous photos of Koko the gorilla raising a kitten? Mother said she felt like the kitten trying to raise a gorilla.

Mother never understood why I did these things, but she vigorously defended and encouraged me anyway. My favorite example of this occurred in my first campaign. She got over the shock of my announcement and threw herself into campaigning. We were knocking on doors together in a Denver neighborhood. She did one side of the block and I did the other. One of the women who answered the door yelled as she walked away, "How can you, a woman, support someone who should be home taking care of her children?" Mother planted her two feet and yelled back, "Because I worked when my children were young, and they turned out great." The woman didn't give up and said, "Oh yeah, what do your kids do?" Mom said, "Well, my daughter is

Pat Schroeder, and am I ever proud." As the woman backed off and I was choking up across the street, I thought, "Now, that's a terrific example of motherly love." You defend your offspring vigorously, even if you can't imagine why they made the life choices they made!

Unconditional Love

CHRISTINE TODD WHITMAN

Former Governor
of New Jersey,
Administrator of
the EPA

Thanks, Mom, for being my best friend and for always having faith in me. Thanks, Mom, for treating me as an adult, allowing me to make my own mistakes and learn my own lessons.

Thank you for encouraging me to try new things, to travel and to learn from and about others. Thank you for insisting that I always be true to myself and the values you and Dad taught us. Thank you for reminding me to always give back to the community.

Thanks, Mom, for showing me a marriage of mutually supportive equals who knew how to be supportive without being subservient, who respected each other and truly enjoyed being together. Thank you for helping me grow up believing that I could pursue any path I chose.

You will always be part of the fabric of my everyday life; the things you taught me are part of who I am. I owe you a great deal, but most of all, thanks, Mom, for always being there and for your unconditional love. I miss you.

Like a Saint

SALLY JESSY RAPHAEL

TV Personality

I didn't want to write about my mother . . . I wanted to talk about her. So I sat down with my daughter, Andrea, and we turned on the tape recorder.

SALLY: I rather fear talking about my mother, because I'm afraid it'll sound like I'm talking about a saint. I can't remember a moment of being punished, a moment of her displeasure, of her not being extremely encouraging, and positive, and saintlike . . . I think it really was that way because I would seize upon any problem if somebody had hurt me.

ANDREA: What's your first memory of your mom?

SALLY: I remember her visiting me at summer camp in Maine, when I was about seven. She was tall, thin, blonde, and always terribly glamorous, looking like the actress Carole Lombard—but in a way that embarrassed me all through my childhood, because we lived in a very conservative town full of very conservative people, and my mother always wore makeup and the other mothers didn't. People would stare at her. She was stunning, and that's all anybody talked about. And, of course, I look like my father. That didn't bother me. I don't think I felt, "Gosh, my mother's beautiful, why aren't I?" She never let me feel that way. She thought absolutely everything I ever did was simply wonderful.

ANDREA: What kinds of things did you do together?

SALLY: Every day was filled with going into New York and taking classes, in tap, ballet, fencing, modern dance, speech or singing class, violin lessons, or the piano. The one thing was that, if I didn't want to do it, she never let me quit. Even if I felt I was the worst violinist ever, I was never allowed to give it up. We worked on my career from the time I was three years old. I didn't think of it as a career; I thought everybody did that.

ANDREA: As you got older, did your relationship with your mother change?

SALLY: When I was seventeen, we lost everything. We went

from a well-to-do family to debt-ridden and in grave trouble because of my father's illness. In America, if you get sick, you lose everything. There was a day when we had to leave town and sell our house, and I the child became father of the man. My father was very ill for ten years before he died and wasn't capable of doing anything. I looked to my mother, and then I realized she was looking to me. From that day on, I became the head of the family, and remained so until the day she died. And she died in a terrible way: A man crawled into her apartment in Florida and brutally raped her, and because of that she had a stroke and never really recovered. We had no money, so we had problems. My guilt is that I wasn't there with her when she died. I don't forgive myself for that.

ANDREA: How did she handle it when your family's lifestyle changed so abruptly?

SALLY: She took it all in with grace. She never thought she was poor, or had missed anything. She did with what she had, and never, ever complained. She was extremely creative in setting up a little apartment for herself right near us, because we were very migratory early in my career. I think my father affected me much more when we lost the money, and I said, "That's never going to happen to me." But I might have worked this hard anyway, I don't know.

ANDREA: Dee Dee, which is what the grandchildren called her, was a very creative woman, wasn't she?

SALLY: She went to the Philadelphia Academy of Fine Arts, Chicago's Goodman school. She was extremely well trained as an artist. In Puerto Rico, she ran an art gallery in a hotel; and after a couple of artists failed to show up at openings, my mother said, "Enough of this," and decided to create paintings herself . . . as five different Puerto Rican artists in entirely different styles! Three of her paintings were bought by top galleries! After she died, relatives descended like the Harpies in *Zorba the Greek*, and cleaned out her apartment. Of the hundreds of paintings she did, I only have three, one of them left half finished when she died. While she was running the art gallery, she was also helping young American girls find safe abortions in Puerto Rico. It was illegal in the United States then, but apparently her name was passed from one person to another, and they said, "If your daughter is in trouble, go to this hotel in Puerto Rico, and go to the art gallery, there's a woman there who will help you." I don't know if it was legal there, but you could get an abortion with decent doctors, not a back alley with coat hangers. She never took a cent.

ANDREA: What kind of listener was she?

SALLY: She was the best listener in the world. The best. Any child who wanted to talk to her could take four hours to say anything.

ANDREA: Did you feel you could tell her anything?

SALLY: Yes . . . although I didn't have anything to tell her!

ANDREA: I have memories of my sister Allison saying, "Let's go and sneak and tell Dee Dee this," because you wouldn't tell her things, you were always trying to protect her . . .

SALLY: Yeah, that's the child being father to the man.

ANDREA: And it was, "Don't tell Dee Dee," but you could tell her, and she'd keep the secret.

SALLY: I changed with Allison's death so enormously that it's hard to explain to anybody who didn't know me before that, but I was very funny then, and everything that happened to me could be a very colorful, heightened, very funny story. I was a stand-up. That stopped the day my daughter died, and I am no longer funny about anything. I rarely laugh at others and I rarely find anything funny. But my relationship with my mother was telling her everything in a very funny way.

ANDREA: She was a very lighthearted person. When I was about ten, Allison and I stayed with her in Puerto Rico, while you were in New York trying to get your career going there. . . . She never said, "Oh, your parents have no money and no job"; she just said, "You're going to have such a wonderful summer vacation with me!" And when summer vacation was over, and we were still there, going to school, she just said, "This is ever so much more fun with you here." Dee Dee slipped so easily into the role of mother, because she was such a good listener and so easygoing. You could talk to her about anything, even sex; she was never shocked. She was always a total fashion plate, decked out with accessories like scarves, fox furs, feather boas. And she always thought everything was easy, that nothing was hard. She refused to take no for an answer.

SALLY: Yes, and she was a party animal! If you wanted to go to a nightclub, that was her big moment. She loved nightclubs, and music, and dancing, and she wanted to be part of that. And she was a terrible flirt!

ANDREA: She charmed . . . she was always raising her eyebrows, dimpling, looking over her shoulder, being coy, fluttering her eyelashes, tilting her head . . .

SALLY: And men just adored her. She and my father never divorced, but after his illness they lived apart. I think love and marriage had been a great disappointment to her. But she was always surrounded by men.

Never Another Like My Mother

CINDY ADAMS

Columnist

Back when we were fashioning my Sunday column, *Post* publisher Ken Chandler suggested I take off on the previous week's events. This idea tapped my creativity because not every week does something momentous happen.

Well, no cutting-edge smart-mouth creativity is required today. This week, something major did happen.

I lost my Mother.

It's tough.

Losing your Mother is tough.

I never loved any creature, big or small, four-legged or two-, man or woman, the way I loved my Mother. And not in this life, or in the many Shirley MacLaine and I may pass through, could I ever love anyone more.

They say a dog gives you unconditional love. My dog, Jazzy, is needy. He makes demands on me. My time, my attention.

My Mom, Jessica—Jessy for short—didn't take. She gave. If I did something thoughtless or stupid, it made no difference. She was always there for me.

One morning, I had no time for Jazzy. When I went to cuddle him later, he brushed me off. Turned his back on me. Unconditional love for me meant Jessy, not Jazzy.

I can't believe my Mother is gone. Even in my heart, the word is capitalized. Every day of my life, from when I lay unfocused and unspeaking in the womb-home she created for me, to when she lay unfocused and unspeaking in the hospital bed I provided for her, she was in my life.

Even in these years when she didn't know it, at least I knew it. I knew somewhere inside that shell was the stunning, bright, sassy, educated, verbal, vibrant, witty, dynamic, fun-loving, killer lady who forever had been my everything, the core of my being.

Maybe twenty years ago, Ed Kayatt, who then owned the community newspaper *Our Town*, had Mom write "A Mother's Day

Message." This week, after days of searching, I unearthed that torn, shredded page. In it, she wrote:

"People told me as my kid was growing up that I spoiled her. I said they're wrong. They didn't understand what 'giving' means or what my kid was.

"She was never the type to take more than one new anything. Now she's grown up and she's the one giving and I'm the one trying not to take more than one new anything at a time."

About ten days ago, when I last hugged Mom in our house in the Hamptons, an icy stab of fear sliced through me. I sensed an increased fragility.

I wanted to crawl into that bed alongside her, but there was no way. No room. And I was terrified I'd frighten her or, worse, the bed would collapse. And so I pressed right up close, my body flat against the protective side bars. All I could do was stroke that small head.

I remember that gorgeous head when it was full of information. When it ruled worlds. When it was big and strong and knowledgeable and featured that powerful mane of thick, reddish hair. It seemed tiny now. The hair white, sparse, shiny.

I was an only child. I married in my teens. So we were four. After my dad went, we were three. Next, my husband. And then we were two. And now I'm one.

Tuesday is the first birthday of my whole life that my adored Mom won't be there.

It's tough.

It's tough to lose your Mother.

So why inflict my own personal pain onto this page? Because Mother's Day is in a few weeks. Storefronts will soon fill with reminders of what to give her.

Last Mother's Day, all I could give mine was a gentle, easy, slow-moving hug. One that wouldn't frighten her. One that couldn't be returned. Or even understood.

Given our frailties, I know there are all sorts of stories out there. In some, the pressures of life have shredded the delicate fabric that weaves a family together. For whatever reason, there are wide, ugly gaps between Mother and child. Not for me to sit in judgment.

I only say, if it's within your ability—call. Tell your Mother you love her.

I wish I could.

I can't anymore.

Turning Challenges Into Adventures

DONNA HANOVER

TV Personality

When I was in third grade, my father, a career officer in the U.S. Navy, was transferred to Guam. My mom wept when she got the news that we would be living on an island that was eight thousand miles out in the Pacific Ocean, which was still full of dangerous booby traps set during World War II; where Brownie scouts sang of Christmas caribou instead of

Santa's reindeer. But in typical resilient style, firmly committed to her family, she did her best. My father went ahead to find temporary housing. So, as Christmas approached, Mom took her three little girls (all under the age of eight) up to Travis Air Force Base for the thirty-six hours of flight on a bare-bones, propeller-driven military air transport plane.

When we arrived, Mom set up housekeeping in a one-bedroom cabin on stilts. We were surrounded by jungle and coconut trees in what was accurately referred to as "the boondocks." We had hurricane shutters instead of windows, a bunk bed on the screened-in porch for the two oldest kids, and a welcome basket from other Navy wives. My parents somehow got us a Christmas tree and brand-new bicycles. Mom learned to play bridge and golf, since those were the major couples' recreation on the island. She dealt with shipped-in reconstituted milk, swarms of mosquitoes, and two years of life on a piece of land that measured only four miles wide and eight miles long. She began the familiar process of relying on other good women for survival tips, baby-sitting exchanges, and strength when their men were deployed on perilous missions for weeks at a time.

What I learned from my mom during our time in Guam is that in life, you need to be flexible, to realize that sometimes difficult challenges are best viewed as an adventure. I learned that living in a civilized way is not about having the finest house or furniture, but about the way people treat one another. I saw that when things are tough, other women can be a great resource of information, strength, and kindness.

As a TV journalist, I now host an internationally syndicated television show called *Famous Homes and Hideaways,* where I interview celebrities in their fabulous homes and visit spectacular mansions for sale. But I have never been in a house that had more deep-down courage and love than our little home in "the boonies" in Guam.

Stunning Diversity

LIZ SMITH

Columnist
and Author of
The Mother Book

Everyone had one with the exception of Adam and Eve. We are either blessed or cursed (or a combination of both), and each person knows into which category his or her perception of or feelings about Mother falls.

In a world of shifting constants, the mother ideal-ideal, the mother dilemma-delusion remains of great importance, holding reflections of the changing times within its encompassing maternal femaleness. We have gone from age-old piety ("All that I am or hope to be, I owe to my angel mother."— Abraham Lincoln) to present profanity ("you motherf——" having been shortened simply to "you mother!").

There is Whistler's mother (*An Arrangement in Gray and Black*) and there is the substitute mother, Auntie Mame (a study in marabou and camp). Barring the advent of Aldous Huxley's *Brave New World*, where there will be test-tube babies and "mother" will be considered a dirty word (the shape of things to come being already here in this instance), the mother bit is a universal experience for animals—a process rendering the female of the species unique, so special that orphans are shaped and traumatized by *missing* Mother.

Whatever one thinks of Mother, whether one loves or hates her, the mothering experience, or lack of it, pays off one way or another. I notice that many great poets emerge from motherless childhoods. They are either early orphans or their mothers are not mentioned at all. It is not so amazing that many of these same artists turned out to be hounded by depression, drugs, and insanity, but did being motherless also drive them to creativity?

Mother often appears in what I hope is some fraction of her stunning diversity. As it is hard to cram Mother into the front seat of the Volkswagen, it is impossible to cram her into the covers of one book. There are miles and miles of books on mothers and motherhood. Just take a look at any shelf 301 in any library using the Dewey Decimal System. Almost every biography and autobiography is a testament to Mother's presence or absence. The literature of Mother abounds.

> A mother understands what a child does not say.
>
> —Jewish proverb

Considering that "Mama" is the first word many of us speak naturally, it's not too surprising that "Mother" has had a tremendous impact on our vocabulary. Nevertheless, it is astounding to learn the wide variety of "mother" terms that turn up in the English language. Some of these occur in an affection context; some are devastatingly insulting. You know all the obvious examples: alma mater . . . mother lode . . . mother tongue . . . mother wit . . . mother-of-pearl . . . mother country (one thinks then of Mother Russia) . . . and so on. One can also get very etymologically complex, and point out that "mama" and "mammary" come from the same Latin root. (*Mamma* is actually a word for milk gland.) But there are many, many more.

By the way of indicating that "Mother" doesn't always mean what one thinks it does, I'll cite the case of a certain small-town librarian who was more than a little bewildered when a prepubescent Cub Scout came to the check-out desk with a book entitled

What Every Young Mother Should Know. After looking at him curiously, the librarian asked some questions. It turned out that the lad was looking for a volume to guide him in his hobby of collecting *moths.*

Joy Marion Sandstedt Snyderman ... My Mom

NANCY L. SNYDERMAN, M.D.

Medical Correspondent and Author of
Girl in the Mirror

When moms were handed out to us in heaven, I was at the front of the line. Some gifts come early in life, and some later. I got one who grew along with me through the decades and the crises in my life. Over the years, we were able to take the magical mother-daughter relationship and watch as it became a true friendship.

There were hints early on that

she was not the typical suburban mom of the fifties. She did some expected things, like giving up a promising career as an artist to marry her doctor husband and raise four children in Fort Wayne, Indiana. But it wasn't a typical doctor's-wife existence. While my father played golf at the local country club, she shunned a country-club life. She preferred her garden, and I was the only kid in our upper-middle-class neighborhood to have a mulch pile in the back-yard. Copies of *Organic Gardening* were never thrown away, and she could sew and repair anything.

She grew up quite poor and wore dresses made from govern-ment-issue fabric during the Depression. Despite constantly mov-ing so her father could find work, she always talked of a happy childhood of picnics and playing outside and exploring. The scrap-piness that allowed her to get through those hard times as a child made her resilient and creative later in life. And she spent the happiness she carried with her from childhood on us, constantly reminding us of the beauty in small things—the crocus pushing its way out of the snow, the animal figures in the clouds as we lay on the grass, and why it was important to be late for school one morning so we could watch our cat give birth. I knew that she was fun and gentle and one-of-a-kind, and she never failed me.

Although she preferred jeans and old tennis shoes to what other suburban moms might wear, she could dress up with the best of them when the occasion called for it. But even a glam-orous woman in an evening gown is her own woman when she cuts her own hair.

NANCY L. SNYDERMAN, M.D.

One of my earliest childhood memories about how truly good she was came when I was eight. My mother was the Girl Scout leader of my brownie troop. (She would soon be the leader of two Boy Scout troops, all three at the same time.) I remember a very poor girl at our school who wanted to be in the troop, but didn't have the money for the twenty-five-cent dues. She lived near school in a life of poverty beyond anything I could understand. The girl's mother's dress was threadbare and dirty, and it must have taken great courage for her even to come to meet my mom. The conversation was quiet and away from the children. I watched my mom put her hand on this stranger's shoulder as they talked. Whatever was said, that little girl became part of our troop and stayed for years to come. I know my mom paid her way, but she never told me, never bragged. There was no reason to do so. Her acts of kindness were done quietly and without fanfare. It is how she has led her life.

She hikes and gardens and has taken care of her health. She has always maintained that a parent has a responsibility to try to stay healthy as a gift to her children and grandchildren. Two years ago, at the age of seventy-five, she got her master gardener's degree and then tended the city's gardens. During her life, she has been a voracious reader and traveler. Once upon a time, she followed my father's suggestions as to whom to vote for, but she found her own voice over the years and has not been afraid to use it. Yet while she has grown intellectually and spiritually, she never lost track of who she was as a little girl. She has found satisfaction in her life and the path that she chose—the stay-at-home mom who raised four good kids who as adults adore her.

More times than not, when I am raising my children, I ask myself, "What would Joy do?" And then I smile and do it. What more could a girl ask for?

The Most
Valuable
Player

**MICHAEL
STRAHAN**

**Defensive End,
New York Giants**

When I talk to my mother on the
phone and I picture her at the other
end of the line, it makes me smile.
We have a casual, comfortable relationship. I call her "Lulu" and she
calls me "Michael Dyckel." We just
have so much fun every time we're
together. When I was a kid I always
wanted to go wherever she went.
Now that I play football in New
York and she lives in Houston with

my dad, I love it when she comes up here to visit. We're like two kids hanging out together. I'm able to do the kinds of things with her that I don't think any of us dreamed we'd be able to do.

When I was growing up, you went by my parents' rules. Whatever those rules were, you went by them. But they were very fair. We had everything we needed, and actually, I think we were pretty spoiled. I can never remember wanting anything. We always had dinner on the table and a nice place to live. I'll never forget the time I wanted a bike that cost about $1,100 and my dad said, "If you're willing to work for half of it, I'll pay for the other half." My parents taught me if you want something bad enough, you can work for it. I think that philosophy still holds true for me today.

Now that I'm an adult, she doesn't interfere. She doesn't get involved with my relationship with my wife—she's never interfered with any relationship I've had. She doesn't give advice unless you ask, and then she'll definitely give her opinion. She raised me to be a responsible adult so that I could handle all my own situations. My mom is very understanding. She doesn't assume, she doesn't accuse. She listens. She's just very rational— she has a very common-sense type of approach to things. My mom is so relaxed—she never seems to be stressed over anything. Even though she raised six kids, she has always been that way. That's why I love to spoil her now.

I love to take my mom shopping when she comes into town. I tell her to get whatever she wants. It's funny because our parents grew up in a totally different time. If someone said that to me, I'd buy everything. She'll go into a store and say, "This shirt is good enough," and I'll say, "No! Get one of everything." I love seeing her enjoying things the way I get to enjoy them. It's really a lot of fun. It's my favorite thing to do when I see my parents.

One of the most important things I've learned is that with all I do on the playing field and all the trophies I've gotten and the awards I've won, the best feeling I've ever had is when I was able to give that stuff to my parents. Just knowing they are proud—especially my mother—is wonderful.

Without her encouragement I would never have been able to become a professional athlete. I grew up in Germany and my parents finally moved to Houston in 2000. When I was in high school there I didn't play any sports. I just worked out. My senior year, my mother and father decided to send me to the States to stay with my uncle so I would have the opportunity to play football. They wanted me to get a shot at something like that. It hadn't even occurred to me. It was one of those situations where they thought it was something that I could do and they wanted to give me every opportunity to do it. They did and it was a huge step. To send their youngest child to another country, not just a few towns away, was a tough decision for my parents to make. My mother was a very big part of that decision. She always checked up on me and encouraged me. It was hard for me to be away from my parents for the first time, but it worked out extremely well.

During my senior year, I stayed in Houston from June to December. By then, I had my football scholarship and I was on the first plane back to see my mom. I went back to Germany and graduated from high school there. I came back to the States for college and went to Texas Southern University, the only school that offered me a scholarship, and spent four years there. Ten years ago, I was drafted as the fortieth pick overall by the New York Giants.

Last year, when Campbell's asked me if I wanted to do the Chunky Soup commercial with my mom, I called her and I was nervous for her. She said, "You better do it! What are you talking about?" It was her first time ever being on television, so doing it with her and watching her have so much fun made it all worthwhile for me. It was one of the best times I've ever had with her.

Being the baby of the family who was the last one in school made my relationship with my mother especially close. To this day, when she's with me she makes breakfast, lunch and dinner. She's still trying to take care of me. She has also been great as a grandmother—she sends out everybody's favorite homemade cookies and cake every month or so. My favorite desserts are her "Sock It to Me" cake, a yellow sponge cake with a hole in the middle and nuts and cinnamon inside. It's incredible! I also love her chocolate oatmeal cookies. My nephew and I fight over them.

We talk every three or four days, even if it's just for a couple of minutes to check in and make sure she's doing all right. I think as we get older, we start to value the relationships we have with our mothers even more. My mom watches all my games and she calls afterward with her comments. She was never one of those mothers who if I was hurt would run out on the field screaming, "My baby! My baby!" That's not her style; she's too shy for that. Her feeling has always been you're going out there to play, do your best, and if you get hurt, that's part of it. When she calls now, she'll ask, "How are you?" She won't say, "I saw you get hurt—you got hit so hard!" She didn't baby us and I appreciate that. A lot of moms would watch on the edge of their seats worrying about that. I think my mom is more on the edge of her seat over how well I'm going to play and whether we're going to win or lose.

The greatest lesson she taught me was to be responsible, respectful, and kind. She taught me to be gentle. That's how I think about my mom—she's kind and gentle, but she's assertive and strong when she has to be. I'm thankful every day for everything she's done for me. She's just crazy, cool, and relaxed—and I love her for it.

A Quiet Strength

ELIZABETH
VARGAS

Television News
Anchor/Correspondent

So many of us strive to be these
high-powered, successful women—
but more than a few of us can also
be reduced to being teenage girls
when we're talking to our moms.
I'm forty years old with a job that
means a lot to me, and my mother's
opinion matters, excruciatingly so—
which can sometimes be a good
thing and a bad thing. It's amazing
how much the mother-daughter

relationship *doesn't* change even as we mature and go through life. She really is still "Mommy" in so many ways. You still always want comfort and advice, and yet you sometimes chafe at what she has to say.

I'm what the military affectionately calls an army brat—my dad was a career army officer. We lived mostly overseas in Europe as well as Japan: the island of Okinawa. Our family has always been very close because every year or so, every single thing in our lives would change, from the country in which we lived to the schools that we attended. A lot of American families stationed overseas tend to stay on the army base, but my parents insisted on getting us out, piling us into the car, and taking advantage of the various countries in which we lived with weekend trips. We learned how to ski in Austria and spent summers camping out on the beach in Italy. It was wonderful.

My mom and I are very different people in many ways—we physically look different. We walk through the world in different ways. But we are both strong . . . and I vividly remember her strength while I was growing up. In a single year of her life, my mom met my father, lost both her parents, married my father, and became pregnant with me. She was twenty. She left Oregon, where she had been born and raised, to follow this dashing army officer across the globe. When the army sent my father to the Vietnam War, my mother was left with two small children—my brother, Chris, and me. She was pregnant with my sister. The government basically said to her, "You've got to go back to the

States." She had no family at that point to go back to, and wanted to stay as close as possible to my dad, so she opted to stay on the island for the year and a half by herself. The military wouldn't let her stay unless she found a home off the base and worked full-time. I was six at the time and the memories of her caring for us, giving birth alone to my sister, and missing her husband fighting a war are still with me. I wonder if I could do it. I am pregnant now, and know how hard it is just to work a demanding job . . . much less all the rest, and in a tropical environment to boot. Let me paint a terribly vivid picture: deadly snakes living in neighborhood walls, termites that swarmed at 6:07 every night till there was no wood left to eat in our house, and cockroaches so big, they would fly. Then there were the typhoons. One was so bad, it knocked down trees and power lines for days. We were trapped inside the house, the wind howling around us, water seeping under the doors and windows, and cooking food on a little Sterno stove. (Truth be told, my five-year-old brother and I thought it was fun!) I shudder even contemplating putting myself in my mother's shoes.

But it's not just my mother's strength that I admire, it is her sensitivity. She can be strong in a way that doesn't run roughshod over other people. She's very, very good that way. I work in a business where people eat each other alive. My mother is a wonderful reality check. She always emphasized the importance of treating others the way I would like to be treated, of showing others respect. I so admire her quiet dignity.

I stumbled into journalism—I hated physics and loved anything literary. But my job quickly became a calling and I developed a real passion for it. My parents were always my biggest supporters, especially when times got tough. My first job out of college, I was very publicly and very painfully demoted after just ten months. My news director informed me he was replacing me with a competitor from another TV station in town, and then proceeded to parade her through the newsroom an hour later, introducing her to all my colleagues. It happened on my mother's birthday in 1985. I remember that date because somehow I held it together that excruciating day until I got home, called her, and burst into tears . . . tears only a mother could understand and soothe.

Throughout my career, my mother has always been my most faithful fan and most honest critic. My parents always cared most about my reporting, my writing, my interviewing, and had plenty of constructive feedback. My mother also had plenty of the typical "motherly advice." "Don't wear that suit again, get your hair out of your face, and be careful not to sound too strident when asking those tough questions." And neither of my parents ever bugged me with "When are you getting married?" questions. That is another way my mother and I differ: my mother was married, with a daughter, at the age of twenty-two. I am a newlywed at forty and pregnant with my first child.

As I contemplate becoming a mother, there are other less dramatic, but truly important gifts my mother gave me. One is a love of reading. Because we lived overseas, I grew up completely without television. Books became my passion, and it was something my mom shared. *Charlotte's Web, Anne of Green Gables,* Nancy Drew, *Gone With the Wind, The Winds of War, Fail-Safe,* and countless others . . . all recommended by my mom, all opened different and fascinating worlds to me. I loved the hours she and I spent talking about them together. It is a gift I hope to be able to impart to my children.

In fact, all her lessons—treating others well, living with dignity, being your best, expanding your mind—all I hope to pass on to my child and to my stepchildren, as well as her greatest gift: her example in setting goals in life high, and her unwavering belief that I could reach them.

Touching
the Ceiling

CAROLE BLACK

Television Executive

My parents were divorced when I was six months old. Mothering was not my mother's strong suit. We lived with my grandparents and she worked in their business. She later remarried and moved away. I grew up in Cincinnati, Ohio, where my grandmother raised me and my older sister, Marilyn.

We called her "Mama," but then again, everybody did. She was mother incarnate and a spectacular human being. My grandparents had a candy store (where we ate up all the profits), and they also owned some rental buildings that she managed. She raised four children and two grandchildren virtually single-handedly. She was quite a role model in terms of being someone who could do it all and do it all very well.

My grandmother was also the kind of person who was supportive in every way. It's wonderful to have someone who believes in you and it's even more wonderful if it's the mother figure in your life. She had very high standards. I can remember something that happened to me when I was in the sixth grade. I was very excited because I loved my sixth-grade teacher, Miss Lingo. When I got my report card I got thirteen As and a B in gym. I had this wonderful evaluation by Miss Lingo about how terrific I was and I was so excited when I read it that I raced all the way home. I ran into the kitchen, where my grandmother was having a cup of tea and reading.

I said, "Look at this," as I proudly handed her the report card.

She looked at it and said, "That's really nice. Why did you get a B?"

I said, "It's a B in gym. I couldn't climb the wooden pole and touch the ceiling."

My grandmother said, "You know what? Next time you'll touch the ceiling."

She always wanted us to do our very best and believed it wasn't worth doing something unless you did it well. Challenging yourself and climbing the pole and touching the ceiling is extraordinarily important. My grandmother taught me the real competition isn't with anyone else—it's with yourself. It's about being the best that you can be—and being exhilarated by that.

When she died at ninety-three, I discovered something. Each of the thirteen grandchildren (including me) thought they were her favorite. She had the ability to make everyone feel very, very special. We all got to laugh about it. In her eyes, we were all very special.

She trusted me a great deal. I was still living with her when my sister got married. I became a confidante—as time went on I wasn't just seeking advice from her. She would share things with me. My grandmother was a person who didn't really believe in gossip. If there were problems in the family she might talk to me about it a little bit. Her instincts were so strong. She always knew the right thing to do.

I divide the world into two types of people—those who think of the world as a place of possibilities, and those who view the world as filled with limitations. She was a possibilities person. Almost her entire family was killed during the Armenian massacres. As a small child she came to this country and could have had a very different attitude. What she said was, "Life is wonderful!" She was always about being fully alive and enjoying all the opportunities we have in this country. She always had a very positive attitude, and I have found that in life, someone's attitude determines how they feel every single day. I loved her optimism and her belief that things were going to turn out well if you did the right thing.

I hope that I inherited some of her wonderful qualities. She taught me to always do what you love and to look at life as a wonderful adventure. She also passed on to me her great love of travel. My grandparents were always going around the world—to Europe, the Middle East, all these different places—and they would come back with amazing stories. It made them broader, more interesting people. I still remember when I was married and we lived in this big old house in Cincinnati. The house always needed repairs and we were told that within eighteen months it would need a new roof, which was an enormous expense. I was going to take a month and go to Europe for the very first time. I went to see my grandmother and told her I was going to cancel the trip because we needed a new roof. At that point she was in her eighties. "Don't cancel your trip," she told me. "You'll find the money for a new roof, but you will love this experience and it will change your life." Here I was so much younger and she was advising me to be the adventurer. She was right, and we had the most fabulous time—and, of course, the money was there later for the roof. I always think of her when situations like that come up, and I remember her advice always to do the wonderful things in life that are good for your spirit and your soul.

She was so proud of me when I would get elected to various offices or win awards in school and always clipped articles out of the paper about them. Both my grandparents believed that as long as you're willing to work, you can do anything you want to do. She was instrumental in helping me achieve my goals. I never had the sense that I was limited in what I could do. I didn't have a planned career but I do think I never limited myself—that just wasn't part of anything they taught me. She made me believe all things were possible.

My grandmother lived to see me work at Disney and was very proud that I worked at the studio. I was then in charge of worldwide marketing for home video, and she was thrilled when some of her favorites like *Cinderella* and *Lady and the Tramp* came out on video. She would have been proud of me no matter what I did.

I think my grandmother is always with me. My sister and I talk about that a lot. We recently went on a trip to Europe together and were constantly saying to each other, "Wouldn't Mama love this?" I was fortunate recently to be inducted into the Broadcasting & Cable Hall of Fame, a prestigious honor in our industry. When I was there I said that I had loved television all my life, ever since the time we begged my grandparents to buy a TV. At the end of the speech, I thanked them. I've been very lucky and met so many people from all walks of life, including some of the most famous people in the world—and my grandmother remains the finest human being I have ever known.

A
Taste for
Life

BOBBY FLAY

**Restaurateur/Chef/
Television Host**

Dorothy Flay is easily the most positive person I know. She is a touchstone for so many people in her life, and without her unwavering emotional support, unflagging optimism, and devotion to family, I never would have made it.

My parents divorced when I was about five years old, so my mother was the primary caregiver for most of my formative years, and she is a true survivor. You see, I was not the most, shall we say, obedient child. I had my own ideas about how I should live my life, and I was a terrible student. Every so often, she would get a phone call from my school saying that I had been absent for four or five days. She didn't know what to do, but she managed like a trouper. I remember one afternoon, I must have been about seventeen years old, and she received yet another call about my absence from school. That was it! She had finally had it and marched down to the corner at Lexington Avenue where I was hanging out with my friends, grabbed my arm, looked me right in the eye (Mom, not in front of the guys), and said, "Bobby, walk. Just walk!" She dragged me home with my tail between my legs. I didn't put up a fight. Why? Because she was my mom and she was in charge.

It wasn't too far from that same street corner that my mother and I had an experience of a different kind. I am a native New Yorker, born and raised in Manhattan. As a child, I used to go to the corner of Seventy-eighth Street and First Avenue to watch the runners in the New York City Marathon. My mother would take me each year, telling me that it was our duty as New Yorkers to cheer everyone on. I harbored a secret hope that one day I would run the NYC Marathon. Not only did I want to run it, I wanted to finish it. Last year I finally ran the marathon. I had several different goals during my training, but my primary objective, in addition to finishing it in a respectable time, was to meet my mother at Seventy-eighth Street and First Avenue. Of course she was there, cheering me on like a madwoman and a proud mom. I grabbed her and gave her the biggest (and sweatiest) bear hug I could manage. It meant so much to me to see her in that same special place we used to go to together when I was a child. It was a very moving experience for both of us.

When I think about why I wanted to become a chef, a lot of the credit goes to my mom, for my first memories of cooking were in her kitchen preparing pork chops and applesauce, Mexicali corn out of the pouch, and my personal favorites, My-T-Fine chocolate pudding and deviled eggs. She was absolutely the inspiration without necessarily being the instruction. She has contributed more to my culinary education than she knows.

Dorothy Flay is one of those special people who everyone, and I mean everyone, loves. She has a multitude of friends and is always the heart and soul at any gathering. She is my greatest cheerleader, with an inspiring spirit that lifts me up when I am down.

My grandmother, my mother's mother, always used to say to me, "Be good to your mother." She has no idea just how valuable that advice was.

My Warm, Loving Greek Mother

NIA VARDALOS

Actress & Writer

My mom and I are really close because she never tried to be my best friend. She's always been my mom. When I was growing up in Winnipeg, Canada, she was definitely the person who said what was what. Today, she's still the one who will say, "Don't try to fit in. Be a leader, not a follower. Be yourself. And don't let them take any more of those sexy photos for those entertainment magazines!"

When I was five years old, like every kid, I turned to my mom and said, "When I grow up, I'm going to be an actress." I guess she thought I'd grow out of it, but because I had a good imagination, she put me in drama classes where I could do plays with other kids. She's not a stage mother at all. She did it because she thought it would be fun for me.

Obviously, I didn't grow out of it, so years later, when I said I wanted to go away to a professional theater school, she was upset. She had encouraged me to do something she never thought would take me away from home. That was difficult for her but she still supported me. I was very heartened by the fact that even though she worried I was entering a life of poverty and rejection, she helped me go to the best theater school and pursue acting as a career, since it would make me happy.

My mother is warm, funny, and very, very wise. I remember when I was young, I didn't want to go to Greek school. She told me I'd be happy later that she was making me go. I went to Greek school from the time I was six until I was twelve years old. Now I love that I can read, write, and speak Greek, and she is gleeful that she was right.

My two sisters, brother, and I play a game with her all the time by asking, "Mom, am I your favorite? Come on, am I?" When we're alone I'll sometimes joke, "Okay, Mom, we're alone now. You can finally admit *I'm* your favorite." She always answers, "You know who my favorite is—Cleo." Cleo was our family dog.

I don't know how she survived our teenage years. My brother woke up at sixteen, decided we were all stupid, and didn't talk to us for the next five years. I don't know how she got through it. My sisters and I didn't take any of her advice for years and now we go to her with everything. It's amazing how smart she's gotten as we've grown older!

My mom worked with my dad—she was the bookkeeper for the various businesses he had—and yet there was always a home-cooked meal for dinner. She's the best at multitasking. You could open the cupboard and there would be a can of tuna and a piece of licorice. An hour later there would be a full-course meal on the table. She's known for that in our family.

We laugh our heads off about how my life has changed since *My Big Fat Greek Wedding* became a hit. She has said she's amazed at how quickly things happened and that she's proud of how I'm handling it. That means a lot to me. She's having a ball with it all, too. She's even talked to the press. One time she picked up the phone at home, and it was a radio station in British Columbia. The announcer asked, "Is this Nia Vardalos's mom?" And she said yes—she probably thought it was somebody collecting on my student loan. They said, "We're on the radio. Can we put you on live?" and she said, "Sure!" I thought

that was so funny. During the run of the film, she was inter-
viewed a lot in the newspapers. Her quotes were really astute
and wisely aimed at marketing the film. She'd say something
like "I'm very proud of Nia for writing a movie for men and
women of all ethnicities." She was just trying to get more people to see it!

When we were trying to get the film made, there were a lot of
setbacks. My mother kept saying, "Everything happens for a reason. There is a reason why this is being stalled." I think about the
timing of when our movie did come out—everyone was ready for
a nice family comedy. She was right about that, too.

I enjoy sharing this whole experience with her. She loves the
stories of who I've met, where I'm going, what each talk show
host is like, and so on. When I had dinner with the Queen of
England, I insisted my parents be invited as well. It just wouldn't
have been as special without them there. When I was traveling
through Europe to promote the film, every time I got to a new
city, I'd call my husband first and then my parents and say, "Woo-
hoo! Hey, Mom, I'm on top of the Eiffel Tower." "Hey, it's Thurs-
day, I'm in Rome!" The first thing she'd say was, "Are you eating?
Are you sleeping?"

The thing I really love about my mother is that she is an optimist. She will always find the bright side of any situation—not in
a naïve way but in a work-through, find-a-solution way. I am so
glad I inherited her Stubborn Greek Girl gene. If I start a project,

you can bet I'm going to finish it. I definitely know my tenacity comes from her.

She taught me to believe in myself, to not give up, to see my ideas through. I'm glad I learned to listen to her advice. The film is a success because of everything I learned from her. I am here because of my mom.

Also Known as "Mom"

JAMIE-LYNN SIEGLER

Actress

Okay, so I think everyone has had different "names" for their moms throughout their lives, through those ups and downs, ins and outs. I'm sure she had some names for me, too. But through it all, she has always been the one that I turned to for everything. Advice, cheering up, a good shopping day, a nice lunch, or just someone to take things out on (which she gladly was on numerous occasions).

My mom was the first person to really believe in me. Especially when I came home that day in 1988 and said, "Mom, I want to be an actress!" I mean, what do you say to your seven-year-old when she says that? Well, if you are anything like my mom, you say, "All right! Let's Do IT!" She did everything she possibly could have for me. Since no one in our family or anyone we even knew was in the business, we had to start from scratch. Well, she found me all of it and more. When I started doing actual shows, she would be there every night. She wasn't the mom that got in the way. She let me have my independence, but it was always comforting to know Mom was in the audience cheering for me. She was my number one fan.

She would brave any type of weather, or crazy schedule, to get me to my audition or my show, so she could be home in time to make dinner and be a mom to my brothers, a wife to my dad. She never complained it was too much. It was always easy for her. Always a wonderful life. Always the best. So that's what it was for me, too. I never would be where I am today without her. She walked me here hand in hand. She was my leader.

During this journey, there was also puberty, first boyfriends, and catty girls. Oh, the joys of growing up. I don't know what I would have done if my mom wasn't there. For as long as I can remember, she always told me to put family first. "Jamie, your friends and boyfriends will come and go but your family will always be here." It took me a while to really understand what she meant, but it is my way of life now. They are my circle of friends. My mom, my grandmother, and I are like "the Three Musketeers." We all share everything. We always find ourselves thinking the same things or calling each other at the same time. She is my best friend.

I remember my first boyfriend. I was head over heels for him. My mom was always telling me, as she did for all my relationships, to make him part of my life but not my whole life. Well, she was so right, but I didn't listen. When he broke up with me, I was devastated. She let me stay home from school, but then woke me up, put on Gloria Gaynor's "I Will Survive," and danced around the room until I smiled. To this day, when I am feeling down, she will call me and play it over the phone. She is my therapy. She even predicted that I would marry my fiancé. I swore she was crazy at the time, but as always . . . Mom was right. She is my fortune teller.

My mom has been through a lot. She had to flee Cuba as a small child, leaving both parents behind. She lived in a country where she didn't know the language and was the victim of discrimination. Going from having everything to having nothing could seem like the end of the world, but once my grandmother came over and finally joined her, they never gave up. They both worked day and night to make ends meet, but their lives were rich with love, faith, and family. That is what she has passed on to me. She is my muse, my guru, and my hero.

My mom has made me who I am today. I only hope that I will be half the mother she is. I hope to pass her legacy from my children, to their children, to their children. Everyone should have a mom like mine.

An Irish Blessing

JOHN MICHAEL
BOLGER

Actor

My mother, Agnes, was born in Ireland and is one of twenty-four children. When she came to this country, she worked as a domestic taking care of ladies and would wind up being their best friend. She'd clean their houses and bring us big bags of secondhand clothes. I was one of the best-dressed kids around. I was wearing clothes with names like "Neil Goldberg" sewn into them—but the garment was from Saks! My father, John, also came off the boat from Ireland with a note and met a labor leader at the time who put him to work at Con Edison, where he stayed for forty-six years. My mother and father met at an Irish dance hall in New York City. He was in the Air Force, and when he walked in wearing his uniform, my mother, who was with my Auntie Maggie, turned to her and said, "I'm going to marry this man." Eight weeks later she did, and they were together forty-six years.

They believed in one another, loved one another, and they gave my sisters and me above and beyond what they had. There were times when we were eating Spam and poached eggs every night, but they gave us the things you can't buy—civility, compassion, love, and caring. They pumped up our hearts.

I was born and raised in the Bronx, the unofficial capital of Ireland, and when I was in high school we moved out to Long Beach on Long Island—the Irish Riviera. I was very fortunate; both my mother and my father were always my best friends. I lost my father four years ago. I have three siblings and my mother has always been our pillar of strength, our rock. She's never wrong. The other day I was at the airport and was standing near a girl who was arguing with her mother and I said, "Listen, your mother is not wrong. Mothers are always right." She looked at me and asked, "What do you mean?" and I said, "Believe me, the older you get you'll see. They're never wrong because they have such an unconditional love for you. You might not want to hear what they're saying, but it comes from a place of love."

I've always been best friends with my mother—we're thick as thieves. We were both born in June, both Cancers. My father and I had a typical father-son relationship but my mother and I have always been major allies. I give a lot of credit to my mother for all the good things that have come to me in my life.

I remember the exact moment I decided I wanted to be an actor. I saw a James Cagney movie and I said, "That's it!" Being that I was the only son, I think that my father would have liked to see me be the president or a priest. For a long time, I never said anything about wanting to be an actor. At twenty-seven years old, after working at Con Edison for ten years myself, I pursued acting. My father, because he loved me, was not happy about this. ("Great, my son is an actor. He's doing plays for free.") My mother said, "Go for it." The greatest thing was when I was in my first play and my father came with a camcorder. They were new at the time and huge. On stage, a friend said to me, "Is that your father in the front row?" I said with a big smile, "Yeah." Afterward, my father said to me, "You know, there was a moment up there when you could have . . ." and I said to him, "All of a sudden you're Otto Preminger."

My mother is very proud of her son, the actor. I've taken her on location with me and people make a big deal out of her, as well they should. She's honest, direct, and compassionate. She's tough and brutally honest. She'll say to me, "You look a little tubby there. Did you put on a few?" I went to Puerto Rico last May and I guess I hit the buffet table too many times. When I came back she said, "How was your vacation? You're relaxed? Good. Now get to the gym." I didn't go back to see her until I dropped ten pounds.

My mother is a great woman. She has these great expressions like so many Irish women do—for example, "Sometimes saying nothing says the most." She'll drop little things on you that always seem to be apropos of what is about to happen. She always just knows. I think when you're that connected to a person—especially your mother, the person who carried you inside of her—they know. I'm an actor by trade and when actors are not acting, they're brooding or they're filling up the reservoir with life experience which will serve them down the road in their acting gigs. My mother will sometimes call me and say, "I know you're lying around feeling sorry for yourself. Get up and get out." I'd say, "How did you know that?" She just knows. She's so in tune with me.

I've inherited an inner strength, a faith in God, and a sense of humor from her. I'm a typical male—I'm forty-six years old and it's taken me forty years to grow up and I'm still honing the skill. My mother (and my father, too) gave me the passport to the universe, which is "excuse me," "please," "thank you," "I'm sorry," and "I was wrong." That's it. You can go anywhere in the world to places that people don't even know what you're saying and you can transmit those things through your eyes. You can look at a person and be simpatico with that person right then and there. You can breeze through a room that way.

I was pretty wild when I was young—involved in drugs, alcohol, fighting, in trouble with the law, the whole thing. My mother and my father (I have to include him because they were one) always told me, "What you're doing is wrong. It's not going to benefit you during the rest of your life." I didn't have the type of parents who when I did something wrong said, "He didn't do it." If I was wrong, I was wrong. They allowed me to learn from my mistakes. That's one of the most important things I learned from my mother. When you're wrong, you're wrong. Admit your mistakes, suck it up, and be a man. I was lucky and blessed to have that. The greatest lesson she taught me is that people are people. Relax, take it easy, roll with the punches. You get more with sugar than you do with salt. It's nice to be nice. My mother is the sweetest lady in the world. She's my heart.

A Brave
New World

**DEBBIE
MATENOPOULOS**

Television Host

My relationship with my mother
has just gotten better as I've gotten
older. We were always close, but it
was a mother-daughter
relationship—I was never able to
see her as a person outside her role
as a mother. I guess in some ways,
when you're young, you don't expect
your mother to be anything else or
have feelings and emotions like
every other woman. I was crazy

when I was young. My brother and sister are older than me and I was rebellious and probably a difficult child to raise. I'm surprised she doesn't have a full head of white hair—she's still blonde and cute as ever. It's funny, the older I've gotten, the smarter she has grown.

My mother and father picked up and left everything they knew—their family, their friends—and left Greece to come to Richmond, Virginia, of all places, because my dad knew one person there. They wanted to give us a better life. I think my mother sacrificed a lot of things, but you take that all for granted when you're young. When I was a kid I didn't realize how much she'd given us and how much she'd given up to make things better.

When I was seventeen I started to go stir-crazy in Richmond—I knew I wanted to be on television. No one in my family had anything to do with the industry. When my parents came here, they couldn't even speak English. My mother went to night school to learn to speak the language, managed to raise three children, and had a beauty salon—and still does. I often think, how did she have the guts to move across the world and start a new life? She worked all day, still had dinner on the table every night for the family, and she and my father helped to pay for college for all of us.

I came to New York City for the first time when I started college at New York University. I was seventeen years old and leaving the nest, which, I'm sure, was scary for my mother. She never once said, "No, you can't do it. No, I don't want you to do it." She always said, "You can do whatever you want to do and you can be whatever you want to be if you believe in yourself the way I believe in you." She never held me back—she wanted me to follow my heart. I think that comes from her and my father doing the same thing. My moving to New York was nothing compared to my parents trekking across the world.

My mother is very, very strong. If I've inherited a tenth of her strength, I will be just fine. She's so strong, but at the same time, she's a very gentle human being. Her exterior is so soft, gentle, and loving that you can't imagine that someone who looks the way she does and presents herself the way she does is so strong. When I was younger I didn't see that, but as I get older, I see that she is the strongest person I know. If it weren't for her I wouldn't be where I am today. It was her belief in me and her encouragement when she told me to stay strong. I really admire her so much.

When I was fired from *The View*, I was in complete mental turmoil. I was ready to say, "I don't want to do this anymore. It's too hard on my heart and my soul." She would say, "Debbie, you're strong. Don't throw in the towel." I wanted to. But she kept saying to me, "You have a gift for this. It's going to be okay. What doesn't kill you makes you stronger. Think about what you have achieved. Don't think about all the bad things. Think about moving on. Forgive them, and more importantly, forgive yourself." My mother would just say, "Remember who you are. If you were able to survive what you did for two years, you can do anything." Now I feel like I'm prepared for anything that could happen to me professionally.

Our relationship is based so much on mutual respect now. I see her for who she is and I understand why she was so protective when I was young. I was so wild, ambitious, and driven. She was always worried that something was going to happen and crush me but she always said, "Go for it. Follow your dreams." She came to visit me in New York and I was living in this shoe box of an apartment. I was so proud of it because it was the first thing I really paid for myself. I had a cardboard dresser that I bought from a drugstore and I had roaches. But she said, "I'm so happy for you." My dad told me she cried the whole way home.

My mother's ability to forgive, her endless amount of love and selflessness—all of that has taught me something that's priceless. She's taught me to genuinely forgive and move on and not to live in the past with the what-ifs. She taught me how precious your family and your life are and not to take any of that for granted. She made me understand that, regardless of the pain, you have to feel all of it to be a whole person. If it weren't for my mother, I wouldn't have this solid ground to build on. She's given me the tools I've needed to work in this business and not be a complete lunatic. Thank you for everything you've done for me, Mom. I love you very much.

"But Seriously, Mom"

COURTNEY THORNE-SMITH

Actress

I once asked you, Mom, what I was like as a baby. You told me I was colicky. I cried all night through many nights of my infancy. You walked me around our apartment for many hours on end trying to quiet my tears and my aching tummy. "Oh dear," I said when you told me about this difficult time. "I'm sorry." *"Finally,"* you said, "was that *so* hard?"

Thus, I learned how to laugh at myself before I even knew how to laugh.

I learned my left from my right from you and our old butter-yellow convertible VW bug, which would start to jerk from side to side as we neared an intersection and say in a wobbly old lady voice that sounded suspiciously like yours, "I don't know which way to turn! Do I go left," as the car would veer slowly left, "or right?" Until big sister Jen or I could force out—through our giggly squeals of laughter—the right answer, the swerving (and, no doubt, the annoyance to other drivers) continued. I learned that pork fried rice and tuna salad is an excellent dinner combination. I learned that the joke is the point, even if it means walking around an elegant hotel bathroom with the end of your holiday skirt tucked into the waistband of your panty hose, as your teenage daughters try desperately not to pee in their own Christmas dresses from the sheer force of their own laughter.

I learned that my dreams matter when you surprised me on my tenth birthday with a day in the "big city" (San Francisco) and tickets to see *The Wiz*, just you and me, because I had shyly admitted a *maybe* interest in acting.

I learned the importance of good nutrition by being taken into yeasty-smelling health-food stores way before organic food was cool or looked like anything more than worm-eaten, scrawny apples and shriveled, hard-as-rocks dried apricots. And later, during a trip to London, I learned that there is nutritional leeway when you looked at me over an afternoon scone, piled embarrassingly high with clotted cream and sweet strawberry jam, and, digging deep into your shortening-rich hunk of white flour, pulled out a lone raisin and said, "I am just having fruit."

When I am with you, I learn that I am way funnier than I actually am, so that after you leave, I spend days feeling disappointed that every silly, moderately entertaining thing I do is not met with peals of laughter and expressions of admiration.

From you, I got my love of reading, movies, and sushi. I learned that relationships are what matter, and it is better to be home with loved ones than anywhere else without them, that six A.M. is the best part of the day, and that my old pets always have a home with you. As do I.

Every time I step off an airplane and see you waiting for me, looking at me like I have the secret to eternal happiness in my carry-on, I learn that I have value, because, certainly, if there is someone in this world who is that ridiculously happy to see me, I must be worth something.

I love you more than words can say, Mom. Always and forever.

Rich
in Family

**LINDA
GREENLAW**

Author of *The Hungry
Ocean* and *The
Lobster Chronicles*

I thank my mother every day for the

sense of family she instilled in me.

Today especially, when I feel like

some social freak for daring to

admit that I love my parents, I am

grateful to my mother for the little

things she told me while raising me.

These things are not new or

profound, but they seem to be

lacking in many of my peers'

upbringings. I do realize that it is

quite unfashionable to admit to having had a wonderful childhood, but I did. It was the best, largely due to my mother. (My friends argue that my childhood has also been very long, and with that I cannot disagree.)

My mother defined "rich" in a way that had nothing to do with financial wealth. I remember bragging to my teachers in elementary school that my family was rich, understanding that rich was a desirable status and one that I should be proud of. What I never felt had to be explained was that my family was rich because we were a loving unit. My mother told all four of her children that we were rich because we had the best father in the world. She said that she was rich because she had the best husband. I grew up feeling quite privileged. I certainly had many friends who were unfortunate in my mother's definition of richness. It was only much later that I realized that these people had far more money than we ever did.

I can't count the number of times during my book tour that someone has thanked me for "not being afraid to admit that you love your parents." I never know how to respond to that. "You're welcome"? A woman introduced me recently at a book event and summarized *The Lobster Chronicles* as a love letter I had written to my family and my community. I liked that.

Parent Personality

MATTIE J.T.
STEPANEK

Author of *Heartsongs*
and *Loving Through*
Heartsongs

Everyone has a unique personality.

That's what makes us different

from each other on the inside, no

matter how much we may seem the

same or different on the outside.

If we all had the same personality,

we would all tend to do the exact

same things at the exact same

times . . . boring, huh? Really!

Being different and unique is an

important treasure, because it

helps shape our lives. Each life is significant. Each life makes a difference. And each life is a valuable jewel in the mosaic of humanity.

I know and love someone very much who happens to have an incredibly unique personality. That person is my mom. No matter where she is or what she is doing, my mom always stands out from the rest. These are some of the key words I would use to describe her: Gracenotes, chocolate, Clean Dish Fairy, news, flexible, dweeb, tea, coffee, computer, loving mother, and optimist.

There are reasons for each of the words I have listed to describe my mom. And I know that there are even more words that could be used to describe her unique personality, but I will begin with this list. The reason I wrote "Gracenotes" is because my mom has something very similar to my Heartsongs. We both record our thoughts and prayers and hopes for life. In some ways they look the same, and in many ways these reflections look different. But in reality, they are similar because they represent our unique spirits in the world through our inner voices.

My mom loves, Loves, LOVES chocolate, so that's why I wrote that word. She doesn't buy chocolate much, but if we happen to have some lying around, it doesn't last long. For example, she always thoughtfully (ha ha) offers to help me sort and check my Halloween candy, especially the chocolate bars. And beware . . . a bag of Peanut M&Ms, no matter the size, doesn't stand a chance of survival once she's spotted it!

My mom likes things neat and organized. She asks me every

morning if I've made my bed and straightened my room. On the other hand, she says she believes in dusting "once a year, whether our stuff needs it or not." And she says that if we put a dirty spoon under our pillows before going to sleep, the Clean Dish Fairy will come during the night and wash all of our dishes for us and even put them away! When we wake up and find dirty dishes still in the sink, my mom sighs and says, "Oh dear, I guess I'll have to fire that Clean Dish Fairy and hope for a new one." I pretend to be upset and say, "No, Mommy, you can't fire her! I'd miss you too much!" Then we laugh and hug, and do the dishes together.

Another thing my mom does a lot is watching or listening to the news. She says that it is very important for us to stay informed about our world, or we can't make a difference in it. She says that the more we know about people and events around us, the more we understand, and the more we understand, the more we can empathize and work hand in hand, or at least side by side, with others.

My mom is also very flexible. She doesn't mind changing her schedule or routine to meet whatever comes up each week, or each day, or even each moment. I get sick a lot, and she never complains about taking care of me, or working at home, or staying up all night to watch me or comfort me. If she learns about something exciting or fun or educational that's going on someplace, she packs us up for a road trip, and we head out for the day. She's busy a lot, but she will always take time for whatever really needs her attention. My mom is very flexible in doing necessary things that range from homeschooling me and attending meetings at work or at the hospital, to playing games and joking around, to making sure we have time to relax and vacation somehow.

I know that the word "dweeb" may sound insulting, but my mom, some of our closest friends, and I have called ourselves the Dweeb Clan for a long time. We each have a funny dweeb name, too. My mom is "Dweebcy" and I am "Little Dweebky." We love to tell jokes and play practical jokes and be goofy. My mom says it is important to know when to stop, but it is just as important to know when to begin. We even have a videotape that we add a little bit to each year called the Dweeb Tape . . . and that name describes the memories on it just perfectly.

When she wakes up in the morning, my mom loves to have a good cup of coffee. On Saturday mornings, I make her a pot of coffee and serve her breakfast in bed. I bring her the newspaper and then we watch some cartoons together. Later in the day, especially on weekdays after school or on a work break, we like to have afternoon tea together. My mom says it's to remember our Irish and Scottish roots, and that it's important to take a few minutes during each day to pause and spend time with someone near us, or just with our own thoughts before continuing in time.

In her free time, my mom likes to work on the computer. That's why I added that word to the list. Sometimes she is journaling, sometimes she is doing work or planning my homeschool activities, and sometimes she is playing computer solitaire games. All of the time, though, whether she is planning or working or teaching or playing, my mom is very caring. She is gentle, she does fun things, she role-models through words and actions, she cuddles, and she listens to me and to life around her. That's why I wrote the words "loving mother."

The final word I wrote to describe my mom is "optimist." My mom is definitely the eternal optimist. She always finds something good in every person and every situation. She believes that we should celebrate life every day in some way. And she has taught me that optimism relies on strengths like patience, and perseverance, and hope. Because of my mom, I know that one of the most important gifts we are given is the gift of understanding. In choosing to use the gift of understanding, we can always find value and connection with all of life.

Each of the words I have listed describes my mother perfectly. My mom is clearly a very unique personality, and she is my greatest teacher. Her teachings help shape my own personality, and because of her influence in my life, I am growing into an honest and peaceful person. When I grow up, I can then be a unique, harmonic person, sharing my voice in tune with the earth and with those around me and around the world. Because of my mom and her unique parent personality, I will be able to influence people to listen to the unique songs in their hearts, which will then help them to shape gentle personalities.

My mom's personality is the type that inspires me, and therefore others through me, to become better people. Although I want to be a peacemaker when I grow up, my greatest desire is to become a daddy. When I become a daddy, I pray that my parent personality is such that I am able to guide my children through life with the same valuable lessons that my mother offered me. And then, the great mosaic of humanity that we are each meant to be a part of will shine brighter with the beauty of unique differences existing in harmony.

With Love and Laughter

KARENNA GORE SCHIFF

Attorney and Child Advocate

My mother let us dress ourselves for school. While other girls were in perfectly matching pink outfits, we would appear in plaid on stripes, too-small, black-hooded sweatshirts, bright flowing gowns, and whatever else caught our eye around the house. There is one photo of my sister holding her backpack while wearing a long brown sequined vest, leggings, and a turban.

Some might think this is some sign of motherly neglect, but I assure you that my mother was constantly focused on nurturing her four children into adulthood. She taught us values, combed our hair, and made sure we had lunch boxes full of nutritious fare (oh, how many times I tried to trade carrot sticks for Twinkies). But she also promoted individual creative expression over rigid societal norms. She wanted us to imagine and dream.

I want to start by thanking her for this gift. Now that I am a mother, I realize how challenging it can be to indulge and stroke a child's imagination, especially while you are trying to just keep them alive and reasonably sane. Our house was a big palette of expression—we built tents in the living room, baked crazy concoctions in the kitchen, and even painted pictures and patterns on the walls of one room. There was an exhilarating freedom to this, but there was also something more—a constant lesson about how to approach life with zest. So many people seem to be trapped in the ordinary, beaten down by the routines of life and the desire to fit in to other people's perceptions of what is proper and right. My mother rebels against that every day.

She has a contagious playfulness and constantly finds little ways to celebrate life. My siblings and I will never forget how she woke us up while it was still dark so we could quietly walk in the first snowfall, and how she taught us to make magic winter treats out of snow and maple syrup. When I was a too-cool participant in a beach party where chaperones were supposed to be way out of sight and mind, she and another mom teased us by walking along the surf wearing Groucho Marx disguise glasses. And there was our midwinter lemonade stand: Most mothers would chide their children into waiting until at least springtime to sell lemonade on the street corner, but I will always treasure those photos of us in parkas and gloves with our Magic Marker sign. I think she was our only customer.

There were certainly times that my mother's imaginative approach to life embarrassed me. After having watched some junior archaeology show, I was convinced that a roof slate I found in our yard was a dinosaur bone. My mother didn't express an opinion one way or the other, but allowed me to fantasize about where it would have come from and how I came to find it. Of course, when I brought it in to the classroom, my theory was quickly dispelled, just as was my insistent belief in Santa Claus and my theory that maybe, if I tried hard enough, I could fly. But even these disappointments contained another of the invaluable gifts my mother gave (or at least tried to give!) me: to not take oneself too seriously.

My mother has an essential joyfulness that has seen her family and friends through many tumultuous times. When my father became vice president and we had Secret Service agents around all the time, she made it seem like a big party. While many instinctively felt stifled or overly impressed by the daunting entourage, my mother was her same earthy self. She learned the agents' favorite foods and songs, played jokes on them (one slightly extreme one was when she put a clump of towels on the

KARENNA GORE SCHIFF

road and pretended that they ran over our dog), and brought out everyone's personality.

My mother treats every person with respect. Whether she is with a foreign monarch or someone begging on the street, she honors the fundamental humanity of each individual. When we were little and we first noticed a homeless man on the sidewalk in Washington, D.C., my mother did not tell us to walk by quickly or look away, she stopped so that we could all focus on who that person was and how we could help him. Soon after, she took us to a shelter to volunteer. This instinctive social activism is another part of my mother's imaginative, passionate approach to life. I want to thank her for sharing it with me.

Finally, I want to thank my mother for teaching me that my sense of self must come from within rather than from what others think and say about me. This is something that she taught through both words and example. When she started speaking up on behalf of parents who wanted warning labels on music that contained sexually explicit or violent material, she was suddenly publicly demonized—people hurled labels at her like "bored housewife," "prude," and much worse. Popular rap and rock stars wrote songs making fun of her, including one that I had had a poster of on my wall! (By the way, she never even made me take that down—another example of her tolerance and wisdom.) Because I was just hitting my teenage years, I thought this was especially trying. My number one concern was being cool, and this was certainly far from cool. But she taught me that there are more important things than being cool, like standing up for what you think is right, not letting the voiceless and powerless among us be bullied, and being true to yourself. Thank you, Mom. The way that you carry yourself and shoulder the burdens of others has taught me much more than I can say.

KARENNA GORE SCHIFF

Portrait
of an
Artist

LEA THOMPSON

Actress

I think the best way to describe my mother is that she's like a force of nature—a whirlwind of strength and change and amazing creativity, constantly reinventing herself as an artist.

When you're the mother of five (I'm the youngest), it's hard to carve out time for yourself. When you have a fire of creativity burning inside, you have to find a way to let it out, and my mother did this by painting through the night. No demands from anyone but inner spirit. She's still painting the night away, saying good morning to my stepfather as he's getting up and she's heading for bed. She's always been so focused artistically—for over fifty years she's been creating: playing the piano, singing, writing songs, painting, sculpting, writing—using whatever she can to express herself.

We grew up surrounded not only by her paintings, but by her acting, lecturing, and performing, too. I think I was drawn to ballet because it was about the only thing she *didn't* do. Then we couldn't be in competition. When I fell into acting, I did different kinds of roles than she had done. She'd always played divas—I started out in the ingénue rules. There was a good voice inside me waiting to get out, but I didn't really start singing until I was about thirty-five, again because I didn't want to compete with her in that way. It's interesting—her talents in many ways held me back, even as she embraced the arts and encouraged us to find our own way creatively. At the same time, one of the hardest things to do is follow in the footsteps of your parent when the prints they've left are huge. I've managed to confront that dilemma and move on.

It helps that Mom is probably my biggest fan, very loving and always supportive of my career. She loves to let everyone know I'm her daughter, and watches all my work. Sometimes she'll offer a suggestion or two, and she's never criticized what I'm doing. That has to be a hard thing for a parent—keeping the support loving and honest. If my children become performers, I hope I can do as well.

Mom raised us with what she half jokingly refers to as "calculated neglect," which meant we did things for ourselves, especially in the poorest times. By the time I came along, I think my mother was burned out with the confinement of traditional mothering, and she didn't have the energy or desire to myopically sculpt any part of my life. When I was almost ten the time came that I had to start listening to my inner whirlwind, and I said I wanted to take dance lessons. Mom told me, "Well, I don't really have the money for it. Here's a quarter. Get on the bus and go get a scholarship." Bless her, it's a whole different world these days. When push comes to shove, thanks to my mother, I know I can go out there and take care of myself, and try the things I want to try.

I didn't always have a full appreciation of my mom's parenting until I became a parent myself. We've gotten much closer; partly because I can better understand how hard it is to juggle the creative "burn" with the rest of life. Being a parent has also allowed me to forgive her for those choices she made, and appreciate how her parenting managed to guide us into being who we wanted to be. While we've always had a strong and loving bond, we have also had times where we drove each other crazy. When I was sixteen, we were having an especially bad time. I remember telling her, "I have to move out because I don't want to fight with you anymore." Looking at those kinds of conflicts straight on has allowed us to have an abiding respect and deep love.

One of the things I admire most about my mother is her continuing commitment and strength as a recovering alcoholic. She's been active in Alcoholics Anonymous for thirty-four years. She divorced my father not long after she sobered up, and the most viable way to support us was to go back to singing as she'd done before getting married. I can't begin to imagine how hard it was for her to leave her kids every night to go sing in piano bars—and not drink.

Even before my first big paycheck, I wanted to take care of Mom, to give her security and comfort and an opportunity to create without having to worry about anything. She's always been gracious about what I've been able to give her. I think it takes a lot of strength and courage to accept my support. She worked incredibly hard through lean and chaotic years. She deserves everything I can do for her. Some people get too proud or too guilty to accept so much. I hear that from other actors, but have never had that problem with my mother.

My mother always says she admires my courage. I feel the same way about her. She's always had the strength and conviction to keep creating. Even when the outside world hasn't been full of encouragement, she keeps on—her paintings are still rich with energy and originality. I admire her perseverance. And if she throws in an occasional bawdy joke, followed by a little blush, or she keeps house as badly as I do, I enjoy those parts of her, too.

In the end, the most valuable thing Mom has taught me through words and deeds is that, no matter what anyone else says, you have to have faith in yourself and keep on going. The most important part of parenting is to be a loving parent. It'll make up for a multitude of missteps and bad circumstances.

Love is the greatest gift a parent can give a child. It sometimes makes me cry to think about how Mom was there for us, always with love and encouragement, even when her life was falling apart; even though she was incredibly talented and didn't get the recognition she deserved. Her courage and her kindness will always be a great inspiration to me.

Simply
Wonderful

**DANIEL
RODRIGUEZ**

Tenor

My mother was a factory worker
all her life—she operated a sewing
machine for the handbag designer
Judith Leiber. When she and
Dad came over from Puerto Rico
as teenagers, they had to start
from square one, learning
English and coping with a new
environment.

We weren't rich, but Mother
made things work—we had things

even when there was no money to have them, and no matter what, she always made time for us.

Coming from a very big and loving family, Mother and her ten brothers and sisters assured every holiday would be a major event. Our family parties were legendary.

Dad was a hard worker, too. He started out as a laborer in a box company and later moved on to a job at the Transit Authority, before retiring. I'm certain I inherited his clown genes. He and I would spend the day seeing who could make Mother laugh the most. Even their divorce during my teenage years didn't change my relationship with either of my parents, because I was always close to them and particularly to my mother.

There was always music in our house. Mother used to sing to us when we were kids. She had one song that I remember very well, "You're Not Sick, You're Just in Love." It was a beautiful lullaby. She instilled a deep love of music in all of us. I have been singing my whole life and my mother always encouraged me.

When I started singing and doing shows in junior high, Mother attended every one of them. In what was to become a grand leap of faith, she allowed me to take singing and dancing lessons with Elliot Dorfman, a teacher at my school and my mentor during those early years. It took a lot of trust on her part to realize I did have potential and to let me go.

If it wasn't for Mother, I don't think my music career would have taken off. I wouldn't have had the training necessary. She sacrificed a lot for us and worked hard to make sure I was given every opportunity.

Mother is my biggest fan. She always knew that I would be, at least in her mind, famous. Even when I doubted it, she was certain. I had been giving concerts every week since I was twenty-four and not looking beyond the obvious that I was giving the gift of music. After a great show, I'd say to her, "Everybody loves it, I get standing ovations. How come I'm not famous?" My mother would be the one to bring me back to earth and say, "Are you doing it for fame or are you doing it because you love to do it?" I'd say, "You're right, I'm doing it because I love to do it," and she'd say, "Well then, you're already famous."

When I sang the National Anthem at the 2002 Winter Olympics Opening Ceremony in Salt Lake City, it was amazing for her to watch me on television. I was so grateful that I was able to share that moment with her.

There is one story that I believe really shows the type of person my mother is. After she left her job at Judith Leiber she started working as a home healthcare attendant. Her sister's mother-in-law was suffering from Alzheimer's; at the same time her sister was very ill, so her brother-in-law asked my mother to take care of his mother. She said, "I'll take care of your mother if you take care of my sister." Although in her fifties, she went to school in order to learn how to become an attendant. She's been taking care of this one lady for the past seven years. My mother lives with her during the week and only gets to come home on the weekends. It takes a truly strong person to deal with that illness on a daily basis. It is a true testament to my mother's goodness and strength, and to the type of woman she is.

My mother has a great heart and bestowed upon me the ability to love people for who they really are. She adheres to the simple philosophy of "Live and let live." The greatest lesson she taught me goes back to our family motto: "Live simply so others may simply live."

It's a simple life—enjoying the little things that make life worth living, not focusing on the big prize but enjoying the ride. That's the lesson that she taught me that has helped me immensely in my career. I consider myself a passenger in a moving car—I let God do the driving and I get to look out the window and enjoy the ride. My mother taught me to always have faith and that all things are possible if you're true to yourself.

Thanks, Mom, I love you.

My Mother, My Teacher

SOLEDAD
O'BRIEN

Television
News Anchor

My parents got married in 1958 when interracial marriages were illegal. My dad is white and my mother is black. They were both at Johns Hopkins University, where my dad was getting his Ph.D. They weren't people who wanted to flout the law—they just felt if they wanted to get married, they would. My mom, Estela, told me that on her first date with my dad, they went to a restaurant and couldn't get served because they wouldn't serve a black woman and a white man together. It just wasn't done. She doesn't tell those stories with a sense of indignation—it's more like that's just the way it was and so we worked around it. Growing up in a mostly all-white town on Long Island, we all did what we wanted to do, and my parents managed to raise a successful family who believed we could accomplish whatever we wanted if we put our minds to it.

My parents always felt that any obstacle could be overcome. Both my mother and my father always quietly but very enthusiastically supported everything we ever did. My mom and dad are very smart and interested in everything—I know if they say an interview I did was good, it was good. If they say it was great, it was great. I respect their opinions so much. In that way, my mother and father have really guided me, but they also let me make my own mistakes.

I'm one of six children—I have three sisters and two brothers. I look back now and think, how did this woman have six children in seven years? My mom is and always has been a disciplinarian. She may have gone overboard in the strictness department—maybe that's just what you have to do to avoid sheer chaos when you have six kids—but she did such a great job of making us feel loved.

My mother and I have always been very close but have gotten even closer as I've gotten older and had children. When I turned thirty, I began to view my mother as a woman and a human being as opposed to just a mother. Now that I have two daughters of my own I have a tremendous amount of respect for her—someone who worked full-time, had six kids, and gave them everything, not in the material sense, but in an emotionally fulfilling way. She always did what she thought was right for us no matter what other people were doing. All the kids in our neighborhood where we grew up went to camp every summer. I was never allowed to go to camp—my mother used to say that was because she loved me too much to send me away. I think my mother fiercely loved—and loves—her children. I have memories of my family doing everything together, including traveling (all eight of us!). My mother recognized it's the time you spend with your children, not what you can buy for them, that's important. That's something my husband and I are trying to emulate with our children.

My mom taught Spanish and French in my high school and was always one of those teachers who was very much respected by her students. She has always been terribly hardworking. My mother has never asked anybody to do anything that she would not be willing to do herself. Something happened when I was in college that made me think my mother was the coolest person ever. At the mostly all-white high school that I had attended, there were few black people. One day I was picking her up at school after she finished work when we saw this young black kid who must have been about fourteen.

He was running through the hallways of the school when the principal stopped him. The assistant principal and one of the vice principals were also there. My mother and I were walking out and we came upon this scene where this fourteen-year-old looked absolutely terrified. In that moment everything was sort of defined for me. Here was this black kid surrounded by these important, powerful people who were clearly making him feel that he did not belong there. My mother walked up to the boy in front of the people who employed her and asked, "What's going on here?" Someone said, "Nothing, Mrs. O'Brien. It doesn't concern you." So she said, "Well, that's okay. I'm just going to sit here and keep an eye on what's happening here." The boy had this moment of incredible relief upon seeing this black lady step in. She didn't say anything, but suddenly the power shifted and the kid no longer looked bereft and alone. He looked at my mother as if to say, "I clearly get what's going on here and you're giving me support. Thank you." When the administrators realized they had an audience, they said something like, "Don't run in the halls, young man" and let him go. At that moment, I thought my mother was the coolest person in the world—she got the whole dynamic of what it's like to feel like an outsider and to have people make you feel uncomfortable. That's my mother—the woman who always stands up for what she believes in even when it's not popular to do so. I hope that I have inherited her ability to do the right thing and stare down people at moments when it counts.

My mother also showed me how important a really strong marriage is. She used to say to us, "I love you all equally, but I love your father the most." Their relationship is a great one—we just celebrated their forty-fourth wedding anniversary. They have provided a great road map for me. My children are my mother's fifteenth and sixteenth grandchildren. As I look toward preschool for my oldest daughter, I am taking stock of what I want for my children. I want my daughters to be happy and self-confident people who love life. My mother and father did a great job of making us feel that way— that life was good, that people could accomplish great things, and that their children could go on and do the same. I think my mother feels her work is done now. She's happy that all her children are married and have found happiness with another person. I truly believe that my brothers, my sisters, and I were raised really well. My mother is exactly the kind of mother I want to be.

The Calm Amid the Storm

KATE McENROE

Television Executive

When I was eight years old I had my first sleepover birthday party. Instead of getting a store-bought cake, as a special treat my mother made the most beautiful cake. She took an incredible amount of time decorating it with fresh flowers. I still remember that cake today. I knew then—as I do now—that my mother was a very special person.

She did things to make each of her children feel special in their own right.

I don't think I really appreciated how complicated and taxing my mother's life was—raising five children (I'm the only daughter), working as a nurse, and participating in my dad's business. My mother had very little help—she did it all. After I adopted my two children in 2000, I was finally able to understand how much care, energy, and attention children need. I am amazed and astonished by what my mother was able to do. Even with five rambunctious children, she rarely lost her temper—she tried to reason with us, and when that didn't work, she used a spanking as a threat. Although I don't believe she ever would have given any one of us a spanking, the threat of one was enough.

Our house was just pure bedlam, but she always managed to stay very centered. All of us had lots of friends and my mother was always open about having other people around. We always seemed to have foreign exchange students staying with us. I remember one Easter we were supposed to have about twenty-five people for dinner. Somehow, the number grew to sixty and my mother and I were in the kitchen and we just started cutting the ham into smaller and smaller pieces. She said to me, "You know, honey, I don't think we should eat right now."

When I was growing up we lived at the bottom of a hill, and once at two o'clock in the morning a car came down that hill and crashed right through the front of our house. We were all screaming, but my mother stayed very calm. She first went to the person driving the car to make sure he was okay and then called the ambulance. Thankfully, everyone was fine. My mother was—and is—incredibly easygoing and remains one of the calmest people I've ever met. There's an inner peace and stillness about her—she's very content with who she is.

My mother always did these incredibly touching things for me. Even though I went through a bit of a rebellious period like everyone else in high school, I remember there were so many instances when my mother showed me tremendous kindness. When I was a freshman I acted in single-act plays at my school. For one play, I ended up sneaking half of our living room furniture out of the house the day before a performance. Most mothers would have gotten pretty upset, but when she came to the play and saw her furniture onstage, all she said was, "I guess this means I'm going to need some new furniture." When I was a senior I was nominated for Homecoming Court and there was a special shawl I really wanted to wear for the occasion that was very expensive. The day before the ceremony she went out and bought it for me. She was always doing things like that for all of us.

My mother was always first and foremost my mother, but every now and then she let me get my way. One summer when I was going away for camp, I insisted on having this bright purple *awful* piece of luggage. Mom tried reasoning with me about why I should be getting the typical camp duffel bag, one that was much more useful and half the price. Well, I hemmed and I hawed about this purple bag until she finally gave in and purchased it for me. Lo and behold, I returned from camp and admitted to her that the purple bag was all wrong for camp and she was right. She never made me feel bad and never once said "I told you so." I decided that I would pay her back by renting it out on the weekends to my four brothers, who of course never took me up on this.

Most people where I grew up in Iowa weren't encouraged to pack their bags and go off to college. Both my parents told me they weren't sending me to college for an "MRS" degree. They wanted me to be able to get the best education I could and learn to take care of myself. I got my undergraduate degree at the University of Colorado, which was about sixteen hours from my hometown—almost no one from my high school class went that far from home. When my first job out of college brought me to New York, my mother and father were so supportive. Every time I picked up and moved for a job, which was quite often when I was in my twenties, they would say, "Go and try it, if it doesn't work out, you can always come back." Now the mobility of women isn't an issue, but back in the early eighties I think only about 10 percent of business travelers were women. Nevertheless, my mother never faltered in her encouragement.

Today my mother is my best girlfriend and confidante. I can tell her anything about anything and there's no judgment, there's just unconditional love. When I became a mother, she began sending a package to me every Saturday with little cards for the kids, tips for me ("Are the children eating the right food groups?"), and books. My son, Christian, has some motor skills problems, so she sent a therapeutic putty she read about for him to play with. Sometimes she just sends a little cartoon she thinks I might enjoy or a picture of me as a little girl. She recently sent me a little red coat that had been mine for my daughter, Caitlin, to wear.

I wish I could say I've inherited my mother's peacefulness, but I'm afraid I can't. I do think my organizational skills come from her, which certainly come in very handy as a single mother with two children. I also see now that she's passed on an unequivocal love for children. I know that my desire to do anything it takes for my children is something that I saw in her when I was growing up.

My mother still offers me the same sage advice she did when I was just a child. She'll say, "You can take a rest, but you can't quit. Whatever you start, you should finish." That's become my motto when life seems overwhelming. When I don't think I can take another day, I know it's time to take a couple of days off, take a walk, or do whatever it is that I need to do and then pick back up again. My mother taught me not to give up and to believe in a higher being and in myself. She is, without question, one of the greatest people I have ever known.

Mamma
Knows Best

**SENATOR
ALFONSE D'AMATO**

**United States Senator
(1980–1998)**

I was born in Brooklyn and moved to New Jersey, where my family lived until I was eight years old. Then we moved to Island Park, a working-class community on the south shore of Long Island. That was when we got our first house, and that's the house Mamma and Pop still live in. I still eat dinner with them a minimum of once a week—sometimes more—and always on Sundays. It's not unusual for me to be there on Monday night, which is our traditional soup night. I've got a great mom and pop.

Mamma has always been incredible. She has been there for the best of times and the worst of times. When I was eight, I was legally blind. I wore these horrific glasses and was the subject of all kinds of taunts from the neighborhood kids, like, "Hey, four eyes!" It was Mamma who liberated me from near blindness. I started wearing glasses when I was two years old and was finally operated on when I was ten. In those days surgery was very risky. The defining moment was when I basically ran into a neighbor's car that was coming toward me on the street. My mother finally said, "I'm not going to continue like this. If he loses his eyesight, I'll take care of him. I'm not going to have him running around like this anymore." So after the surgery, I discovered a whole new world. I could read!

At the time, I was the little Italian kid in the new neighborhood. The one thing my mother always taught me was to stand up and be a fighter. She used to tell me, "Sticks and stones may break your bones, but names will never hurt you," but that's not true when you're a kid. I became rather fierce for my age and size—because I knew that's how people come to respect you. That was because of Mamma—she is a fierce spirit.

Our close relationship was born out of my being somewhat fearful of falling into Mamma's doghouse. While she taught me to stand up for myself and to stand up for other people, she also taught me that there were consequences when you didn't do something you were supposed to do. I'll never forget when I was in the seventh grade and the principal called me in for something. Mamma was so embarrassed that she chased me around the house with one of my books. I became very mindful that I should never embarrass Mamma again.

We were a family of modest means, but we never knew it; we had a great time. She was an incredible homemaker who kept our family together. In her early days of marriage, when Pop went into the army during World War II, she worked on the assembly line in an aircraft factory. Mamma created a wonderful environment so that my friends always loved to be around her, from the time when I was a kid, through my college days (my friends always raided her care packages when they arrived for me at Syracuse University!), and it still continues now. Forget about having people come to the house to see me; they come for Mamma's wonderful meals. [Former New York City] Mayor Koch loves to come to Mamma's for dinner. My Senate friends and I have a tradition. We have a club—The Wednesday Group— where one senator hosts twenty-five to thirty senators for lunch a couple of times a year. When my turn came, Mamma would come down with big tins of lasagna. To this day, my senator friends ask me, "When is Mamma coming?" She proudly displays a proclamation in her kitchen that some of the guys, Senator John Warner and a few others, made for Mamma's great food.

My mother has a complete and total devotion to her family as well as a fierce determination to challenge them to do the best they can and to stand up and take full advantage of getting a good education. My sister got a master's degree in literature; my brother went to law school. She taught us never to be afraid of expressing ourselves and to go out and become involved. My mother was totally committed to giving her family every opportunity. When she was growing up, education for women in particular was not something that was readily available, but she made up for it. She was a great reader. Her own dad never encouraged her, so she made sure her daughter and sons had those opportunities.

Mamma believed you could do whatever you wanted to do if you were willing to pay the price—giving up leisure time to pursue something, whether it was academics or a professional choice. If you were willing to do that, you could succeed. She always told us to do our best because it's the right thing to do. Today I believe there isn't anything you can't achieve if you're willing to pay the price. It doesn't mean if you want to run for president you're guaranteed to become president, but it does mean you can make a significant contribution in the public arena if that's what you choose. I remember when I told her I was going to run for the Senate.

My father asked, "You're going to run for *what?*"

I said, "The United States Senate."

He said, "Son, you should run to see a psychiatrist."

Mamma said, "Oh, I think that's nice."

When the 1980 campaign started out, I was trailing in the

polls. My mother took to the campaign trail with me and did a commercial that turned it all around. In the ad she was carrying her groceries and talking about how things were difficult for young middle-class families. Then just before she went into the house with her groceries she said, "Vote for my son, Al; he'll be a great senator." It was just incredible. Then she went on the road and she even had a booklet of her inflation-fighting recipes. Some of the newspapers wanted to know if the recipes were real or not, so the New York *Daily News* tested them and found out they were great! She enjoyed campaigning—it was like her coming out. There wasn't anybody who worked harder. She traveled throughout New York State. People turned out just to see her and she had this wonderful way with them. Someone would try to ask her about my position on a certain issue and she would say, "I'm not here to talk about that. He's a good person." She was disarming and charming. Boy, does she know people. Her instincts are second to none. There's no doubt in my mind between the commercials and her appearances, she made the difference. She instilled a real sense of pride in the Italian-American community.

Mamma also taught me something else that has been indispensable to me during my political career. Don't be afraid to be criticized, she said. If you are, so what? Take it from where it comes. I'd get bent out of shape. She'd say, "Forget about it. Just do what you have to do." I also learned that when you make a mistake, own up to it. Today politicians lose and they blame it on their campaign manager. Baloney! Mamma taught me no one is entitled to anything—it's up to you, and if you think that everything is fair, it's not. Get over it. Don't cry.

The little dynamo stands about five foot one. She's always saying, "I wish my legs were longer so I could be at least five-six." To me, she is larger than life itself. There's no one in the world like Mamma.

Thanks to
My Own
Mom